GIT Testing Agile DevOps SAP S/4HANA Top 500 PLUS Interview Questions and Answers

By
Sudipta Malakar

Acknowledgement

No task is a single man's effort. Cooperation and Coordination of various people at different levels go into successful implementation of this book.

There is always a sense of gratitude, which everyone expresses others for their helpful and needy services they render during difficult phases of life and to achieve the goal already set.
At the outset I am thankful to the almighty that is constantly and invisibly guiding everybody and have also helped me to work on the right path.

I am son of Retired Professor (*Shri Ganesh Chandra Malakar*). I am indebted to my Father as without his support it was not possible to reach this Milestone. My loving mother (*Smt. Sikha Malakar*) always provides inspiration to me. My cute loving Son (*Master Shreyan Malakar*) is always providing me precious support at his level best.

I am thankful to my parents, spouse, son, family and my Sirs (Mr. David J Anderson, Creator of Kanban Method and CEO, David J Anderson School of Management, Mike Cohn, CST, Nanda Lankalapalli CST, Peter Stevens, CST, Abid Quereshi, CST, Brian Tracy, CEO of Brian Tracy International) for their guidance which motivated me to work for the betterment of consultants by writing the book with sincerity and honesty. Without their support, this book was not possible.

Finally, I thank everyone who has directly or indirectly contributed to complete this authentic work.

PREFACE

Certified Agile Practitioners or Certified Testing Practitioners or Certified S/4HANA SAP Practitioners are on high demand. Organizations seeking to adopt a more agile method or SAP S/4 HANA now always choose Scrum or KANBAN as their framework. Thus, a large part of the team's success depends on a skilled Professionals. It is on their hands to make a difference in the dynamics and performance of an agile team. Whether you are new to Scrum / KANBAN / DevOps or already an expert, it is always beneficial to know how to prepare for a job interview in this field.

Nervous about your interview? You are studying day and night. But still you are very nervous. How to crack the JOB interviews?

This book uncovers the different areas under which questions are asked and what are the most commonly asked ones. We hope that these will help you while preparing for your Job interview.

The examples given in book are user-focused and have been highly updated including topics, figures, strategies, best practices and real-life examples, demos and case studies.

This book promises to be a very good starting point for beginners and an asset for those having insight towards Agile, DevOps, Testing Automation, SAP S/4 HANA and Technical best practices.

It is said **"To err is human, to forgive divine".** Although the book is written with sincerity and honesty but in this light, I wish that the shortcomings of the book will be forgiven. At the same the author is open to any kind of constructive criticisms and suggestions for further improvement. All intelligent suggestions are welcome and the author will try their best to incorporate such in valuable suggestions in the subsequent editions of this book.

Table of Contents

Introduction

Certified Agile Practitioners or Certified Testing Practitioners or Certified S/4HANA SAP Practitioners are on high demand. Organizations seeking to adopt a more agile method or SAP S/4 HANA now always choose Scrum or KANBAN as their framework. Thus, a large part of the team's success depends on a skilled Professionals. It is on their hands to make a difference in the dynamics and performance of an agile team. Whether you are new to Scrum / KANBAN / DevOps or already an expert, it is always beneficial to know how to prepare for a job interview in this field.

Nervous about your interview? You are studying day and night. But still you are very nervous. How to crack the JOB interviews?

This book uncovers the different areas under which questions are asked and what are the most commonly asked ones. We hope that these will help you while preparing for your Job interview.

This book promises to be a very good starting point for beginners and an asset for those having insight towards Agile, DevOps, Testing Automation, SAP S/4 HANA and Technical best practices.

To make clarity of the programming examples, logic is explained properly as well discussed using comments in program itself. The real-time examples are discussed in detail from simple to complex taking into consideration the requirement of IT consultants. Various sample projects are included in the book and are written in simple language so as to give IT consultants the basic idea of developing projects in Agile & DevOps. The examples given in book are user-focused and have been highly updated including topics, figures, strategies, best practices and real-life examples, demos and case studies.

The book features more on practical approach with more examples covering topics from simple to complex one, addressing many of the core concepts and advance topics also.

The book is divided into the following sections:
- 500 PLUS Real-time GIT, Testing, SAP S/4HANA, Agile & DevOps interview questions and answers
- Numerous Tricky Real-time SAP S/4HANA, Agile & DevOps Case Studies and Demos
- Stakeholders Agile Survey questions
- Common Agile Product Development & Test Automation Myths
- Service Oriented Architecture, Client Server Architecture, 4+1 Architecture View Model
- Infrastructure as a Service (IaaS), Platform as a Service (PaaS), Software as a Service (SaaS)
- DevOps Implementation – Approach & Guidelines

- Agile Budget Management
- Agile Contract Management
- Technical best practices
- Change Management Process - DevOps
- Quality Management Process - DevOps
- Get to know what are continuous integration, continuous delivery, and continuous deployment
- Agile & DevOps main goal and challenges
- Integrate recent advances in DevOps and process design strategies into practice according to best practice guidelines
- Software development and Agile

Chapter 1 - Introduction

Agile began as an iterative, collaborative, value-driven approach to developing software.

It was originally conceived as a framework to help structure work on complex projects with dynamic, unpredictable characteristics.

But since then, it has evolved into somewhat of a philosophy or world view, with a set of well-articulated values and principles common between Agile's many varieties.

1.1. Agile Interview questions and answers

1.1.1. What are the reasons to take an Agile Certification?

- Agile certified consultant can deliver project and product as per end user perspective.

- Agile certified consultant can deliver project and product in incremental & iterative way. He/she can adhere to extreme programming & lean principles (as applicable).
- Agile certified consultant can deliver project and product to maximize ROI. Agile certified consultant can maximize the stakeholders delight by gaining in-depth knowledge in Agile.
- Scrum / Agile certification is must to deliver work with best team velocity / productivity. Agile certified consultant can maintain good first-time right products quality. Here, the teams are self-organized, cross functional.

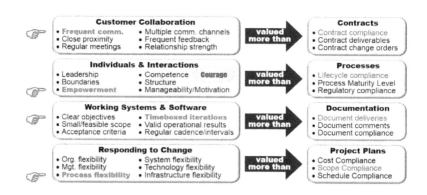

Figure 1.1: Agile Manifesto illustration

- To get more salary and getting promotion Agile Certification is the must
- Agile certified consultant can get different tips & traps in Agile Project Management. You can get different delivery management strategies and tips on customer centric focus. It helps him / her to create transparency at workplace via different Scrum ceremonies.
- Agile Certification helps consultant to stay aligned with current industry trends. Agile Certification helps consultant to adhere to best practices.
- After agile certification you can become Agile community member. Thus, you can enhance your skill sets by iteration with your peers. You can inspect, adapt through transparent continuous feedback loops.
- Agile certified consultant can act as a change agent. He/she can drive organizational change.
- Agile certification helps consultant to improve their skill sets in different techniques, servant leadership.
- Agile training and certification help consultant for facilitating stakeholder discussion, road mapping. It also helps him / her for product discovery.
  It also helps him/her improving and managing the product backlog, product management. Agile certified consultant can also perform effective release planning.
  Agile certified consultant can do effective implementation of engineering practices, technical debt.
- Sometimes volume of work is unpredictable. Often bottleneck situation arises. Then it is very tough for the consultant to handle it.
  But Agile certified consultant can manage the flow of work. He / she can do mapping between customer demand and supply.
- Agile certified consultant can manage project and product with good quality. Agile certified consultant can deliver projects as per signed SLA or KPIs. He/she can deliver products through incremental & iterative shippable products delivery. He/she can abide by Agile / scrum and Lean values, principles, and worldview.
  It helps him/her to focus on quick response to the proposed changes. It comprises short duration iterations.
- Agile training and certification help consultant in scaling Organizational development, Conflict resolution. It also helps consultant in Agile facilitation and coaching.

- Agile certified consultant can find creative ways to help organizations. He/she can help his/her peers to adopt the Agile framework and capitalize on its benefits.

Be the change YOU want to see...

Roll up your sleeves and show them how it's done.

- Mahatma Gandhi

Choosing a certification that is best for you doesn't lead to the success that you deserve. The effectiveness of the course depends on the training provider.

So, always choose for Agile certification based on your experience.

1.1.2. What is PMI-ACP® certification

Project Management Institute (PMI) offers **Agile Certified Practitioner (ACP)** certification. It is for professionals currently using agile or are moving to agile practices.

Team leads, project leads or for leadership professionals can attend this certification.
It is also for *Being Agile* practitioners following daily agile principles and methodologies.

1.1.3. Benefits of PMI-ACP® certification

    a. Agile Certified Practitioner can apply Agile principles and values in different Agile methodologies. Like SCRUM, XP, Lean, KANBAN, and so on. So, it gives them better visibility.

    b. Better salary as the salary of a certified PMI ACP professional is about 28% higher than that a non-certified professional.

    c. Agile Certified Practitioner can perform as Change agent in continuous improvement initiatives. Thus, they can add values in their organization. So, it increases their credibility.

    d. Keeping up to current market trends.

    e. To manage the projects in an effective way as *Being Agile*.

    f. If your organization is looking forward to introduce Agile framework for achieving high end project goals, then PMI ACP certification is best to choose.

    g. Agile Certified Practitioner can do Agile risk management

    h. Agile Certified Practitioner can do Agile value stream analysis, value based prioritization

    i. Agile Certified Practitioner can do RCA using different statistical methods like five WHYs, fishbone diagram analysis.

    j. Agile Certified Practitioner can plan and manage Agile KPIs.

    k. Agile Certified Practitioner can plan and manage Agile Metrics.

    l. Agile Certified Practitioner can follow and drive Agile Manifesto, principles, values, tools, techniques in projects.

1.1.4. What is SAFe® Agilist

A Certified SAFe® Agilist practitioner is a lean agile change agent in large IT organization while working with multiple teams.

1.1.5. Benefits of SAFe® Agilist

    a. Better visibility, as a Certified SAFe® Agilist practitioner can apply Lean-Agile Mindset and principles.

b. Better salary, as the salary of a certified SAFe Agilist professional is about 30% higher than that a non-certified professional.
c. Certified SAFe® Agilist practitioner can drive many value added activities in an organization. So, it increases their credibility.
d. Keeping up to current market trends.
e. A Certified SAFe® Agilist practitioner can manage portfolios of agile teams and can do lean agile budgeting.
f. A Certified SAFe® Agilist practitioner can plan and execute program increments.

SAFe Agilist and Scaled Agilist terms are synonyms. This is the position given to a person who has completed the course Leading SAFe. The two-day informational course and certification exam which creates the following outcomes:

- Successful application in Agile enterprise environments.
- Recognition of Lean-Agile mindset.
- Development and empowerment of consultants through Lean portfolio.
- Support of Agile leadership principles. It drives itself to organizational transformation.
- Continuous iterative incremental cycle of continuous improvement. You can use dot voting technique for this.

1.1.6. PMI-ACP® vs. SAFe® Agilist : Key Differentiators

Sr. No.	Description	PMI-ACP®	SAFe® Agilist
1	Training	It requires 21 Professional development units PMI ACP training. It can be classroom or online training from **Registered Education Provider (R.E.P.)**	It is mandatory to attend two days SAFe agile certification classroom training. The course covers SAFe defined content by training providers.
2	Certification Course Fee	- PMI ACP certification cost for online self learning is $400. - PMI ACP certification cost for live online training is Rs. 34930. Visit the site to have detailed info about PMI ACP certification course. **PMI ACP certification provider URL –**	Various worldwide vendors provide the SAFe agile training and it costs around $1,000. Visit the site to have detailed info about SAFe agile certification course. **SAFe Agilist certification provider URL –** https://www.scaledagile.com/certificatio n/which-course-is-right-for-me/

		https://www.greycampus.com/pmi-acp-training-instructor-led	
3	**Experience /Eligibility/ Prerequisites**	a. 2000 hours or 12 months of real-time project experience (earned in last five years) in managing project teams. b. Additionally, 1500 hours or 8 months of real-time Agile project experience (earned in last three years) with agile methodologies. c. 21 hours of Agile training in agile methodologies, values, lean agile principles, practices, tools and techniques. d. Secondary degree (associate's degree or high school diploma or global equal).	a. Five plus years' experience in business analysis, testing, software development, project or product management. b. Experience in SAFe SCRUM. He / She ensures scrum team's adherence to *Scrum* during agile projects.
4	**Exam Cost**	For PMI member agile certified practitioner PMI ACP certification cost is $435.00 (Computer based exam fee). For Non PMI member agile certified practitioner PMI ACP certification cost is $495.00 (Computer based exam fee). And, Paper based exam fee is: - $385 for PMI member, - $445 for Non PMI member.	Safe agile certification cost is $995 per course. Here first exam attempt is free.

5	**Course Content**	Agile project management training course table of contents include the following: - Many Agile methodologies like SCRUM, XP, Kanban, Lean. - Agile Manifesto, principles, values, tools, techniques - Scrum artefacts, roles, ceremonies, - Estimation techniques, Agile planning, monitoring and adapting, - Agile risk management, - Agile Metrics, - Agile value stream analysis, value based prioritization, - Agile product quality, - Communication, - Interpersonal skills. - Process improvements, Kaizen - Statistical methods like five WHYs, fishbone diagram analysis - Agile Contracting - Agile Project chartering - Agile hybrid models - Managing with Agile KPIs. **Agile Project Management certification exam** - 120 objective type questions to answer in three hours duration.	SAFe certification training course table of contents includes the following: - Apply Lean-Agile Mindset and principles. - Plan and execute Program Increments. - Execute and release value through Agile Release Trains. - Build an Agile portfolio with Lean-Agile budgeting. - Apply DevOps principles - Apply SAFe principles for Product owner - Apply SAFe principles for Scrum master **SAFe agile certification exam** - 45 objective type questions to answer in 90 minutes duration - Passing score is 34 out of 45, i.e., 75% is the SAFe certification passing score.
6	**Certification Validity & Renewal**	- Earn 30 **Professional development units (PDUs)** in every 3 years.	You need to renew SAFe Agilist certification or scaled agile certification every year by paying renewal fee $100.

		- Renewal of PMI ACP certification needs to be done in every 3 years. - Renewal fee is $60.	
7	**Course Accreditation**	**Project Management Institute (PMI)** offers it.	Scaled Agile offers it.
8	**Salary**	The salary of a certified PMI ACP professional is about 28% higher than that a non-certified professional.	The salary of a certified SAFe Agilist professional is about 30% higher than that a non-certified professional.

1.1.7. How to judge the Agile Certification which is a best fit for your career

- It's 3 steps approach.
- Choose the Agile Certification which is best fit for purpose of your career path and as per your current job role & skill sets.
- We can correlate it in the below three step approach to choose the best Agile certification as per your current career path.

Figure 1.2: How to choose your Agile certification

1.1.8. Conclusion

Team leads, project leads or for leadership professionals can attend this certification.
It is also for *Being Agile* practitioners following daily agile principles and methodologies.
PMI-ACP certified consultant helps your company for achieving high end project goals.

PMI-ACP® Exam is not limited to Scrum Framework. It also includes other frameworks like Lean, Kanban, and XP. PMI-ACP® is strong examination compared to the basic Scrum Master certifications. You also need to take a classroom or online training before appearing in the exam.

SAFe Agilist could be an ideal choice for you if you are working with many teams in the adoption of Scaled Agile Framework in your enterprise.

SAFe Agilist and Scaled Agilist terms are synonyms. This is the position given to a person who has completed the course Leading SAFe.

Finally, it's imperative that a PMI Agile Certified Practitioner's role is more of a Leadership role. While SAFe Agilist's duties include more of facilitating and coaching role, the choice is yours, which certification to choose. It is in line with the capability you would like to grow in your professional life.

Choosing a certification that is best for you doesn't lead to the success you deserve. The effectiveness of course depends on best training provider. So, always choose based on your experience.

1.1.9. Top 150 Plus Scrum Master Interview Questions and Answers

Certified Scrum Masters are on high demand. Organizations seeking to adopt a more agile method now choose Scrum as their framework. Thus, a large part of the team's success depends on a skilled Scrum Master. It is on their hands to make a difference in the dynamics and performance of an agile team. Whether you are new to Scrum or already an expert, it is always beneficial to know how to prepare for a job interview in this field.

This article uncovers the different areas under which questions are asked and what are the most commonly asked ones. We hope that these will help you while preparing for your Scrum Master interview.

First, to shed some light on the subject of discussion, let's begin explaining the importance of Scrum certifications. We will then discuss a few tricky Scrum Master interview questions and best answers.

1.1.11. So, what is Scrum?

Scrum is a methodology based on agile principles, with the goal of allowing a team to organize better and be ready to change quickly. It emphasizes teamwork, communication, and speed across complex projects. The Scrum Master is the one who manages the process of how information is exchanged.

Scrum is a process framework for new product development created by Jeff Sutherland and Ken Schwaber. The word "Scrum" is taken from Rugby game where the team huddle is called Scrum. Since new product development is very complex, Scrum offers an iterative and incremental development approach. In Scrum there are 3 roles namely, ScrumMaster, Product Owner and Development team of size 3 to 9. All three roles are empowered to do their job and have no authority on each other. However, they work as self-organizing team to deliver a product with complimenting skills.

Scrum is an Empirical process which is used for solving complex problems like Software Development. Since we cannot predict the outcome upfront, the team goes iteratively and learn and improve in each iteration. For the team to continuously learn and improve, they keep all the artefacts transparent and frequently inspect and adapt.

1.1.12. Why would I need a Scrum Master certification?

A Scrum Master certification demonstrates the core knowledge of the Scrum process. It is an added advantage as it proves the holder as a continuous learner. It shows ambition, which boosts professional growth. These are a few benefits of getting a Scrum certification:

- It provides with Scrum principles and skills.

- It prevents challenges and obstacles which may occur while using an Agile platform.

- It enhances team collaboration.

- It brings a change of mindset for the whole team.

With the growing demand for Scrum Masters, holding a certification adds a competitive advantage and builds a stronger professional credibility.

1.1.13. SCRUM Nuts and Bolts

Here are a few frequently asked questions that will help you prepare for your job interview:

1.1.14. Who is a Scrum Master?

The Scrum Master is responsible for supporting and promoting the Scrum. They assist their team in meeting their goals. They help managing project risks and mentor the team as its coach. The Scrum Master is also known as a servant leader, as they provide collaboration and motivate the team to deliver their best.

ScrumMaster is a Scrum process champion who teaches, coaches, mentors Product Owner and Development team so that they can deliver a product in Scrum process. ScrumMaster's main responsibility is to remove any impediments PO and Development team have so that they can deliver high value and high quality products.

1.1.15. What is a "user story" in Scrum?

A user story is a tool used in Agile software development that captures the description of a feature from an end-user perspective. It describes, among others, the type of user and their motivations. A user story creates a simplified description of a user's requirements.

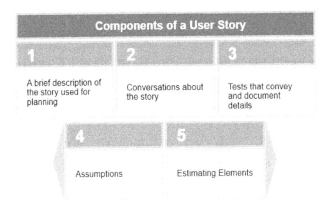

Figure 1.3: Purpose of a user story

A User Story describes functionality that will be useful to a stakeholder of the system.

User Stories - Example

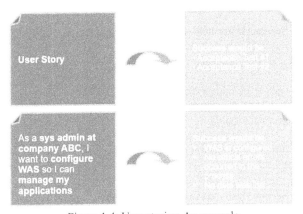

Figure 1.4: User stories: An example

1.1.16. What are the three main artifacts of the Scrum process?

- Product Backlog

- Sprint Backlog

- Product Increment

1.1.17. What do you understand by the term Scrum Sprint? What is its duration?

A Scrum Sprint is a repeatable cycle during which the work is completed and made ready for review. The duration of the Scrum Sprint depends on the size of the project and the team working on it. Generally, it is under 30 days.

1.1.18. Describe the role of a Product Owner.

The Product Owner focuses on the success of the product, ensuring the business value of it. Their main responsibility is to identify and refine the Product Backlog items.

Product Owner(PO) collaborates with customers (users) of the product being developed and understand their needs. Product Owner creates list of customer needs in a Product Backlog and always keeps it in the order of business value. This way PO makes sure that latest needs of the customer are delivered by the development team. Product Owner is also responsible for effective Product Backlog management, helping development team to build the high value product and perform long term planning and tracking. Product Owner is responsible for success of the product.

1.1.19. How does the Scrum Master help the Product Owner?

- Efficient Product Backlog management

- Helping the Scrum team in adopting a shared vision

- Understanding and practicing agility

- Facilitating Scrum events as requested or needed

1.1.20. How does the Scrum Master serve the organization?

- Helping in Scrum adoption.

- Acting as an Agile change agent.

- Helping the team, increasing productivity.

- Ensuring the iterative incremental cycle of continuous improvement. The *dot voting* technique is often used for this.

- Supporting Agile leadership principles, leading to organizational transformation.

1.1.21. Why is Agile methodology necessary?

- It helps achieving customer satisfaction with the rapid delivery of useful software.

- It eases potential changing requirements, even late in a company's development.

- Repeatedly delivers a working software, the main measurement of progress.

- It provides close, daily cooperation between the company and the developers.

- Having self-organizing teams brings as a result self-motivated team members.

- In situations of co-location, it assists communication through face-to-face conversations.

- It offers continuous attention to XP.

- It adds simplicity.

1.1.22. Explain Scrum overview

- Scrum is a processed framework meant to help teams develop projects in an iterative, incremental manner. The process is organized in cycles of work called *Sprints*.

- These cycles do not last more than four weeks each (usually two weeks) and they are *timeboxed*. This means they end on a specific date whether the work has been completed or not. They are never extended.

- At the beginning of each Sprint, the team chooses one of the project's tasks from a prioritized list. They agree on a common goal of what they believe they can deliver at the completion of the Sprint, something that is tangible and realistic. During the Sprint, no additional tasks should be added.

- The team meets every day to review their progress and adjust the steps needed to complete the remaining work.

- At the end of the Sprint, the team reviews the work cycle with the stakeholders and shows the end product. With the feedback they get, they plan the next Sprint.

- Scrum emphasizes on obtaining a working product at the completion of each Sprint. When talking about software, this means a system that is integrated, tested, end-user documented, and shippable.

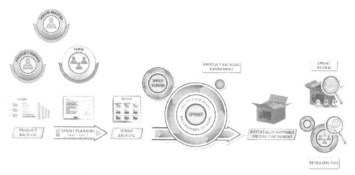

Figure 1.5: SCRUM Process in a nutshell

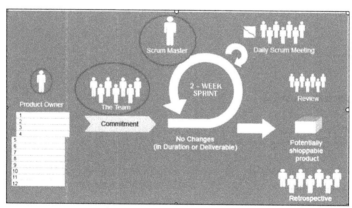

Figure 1.6: SCRUM in a nutshell

Product is delivered in short iterations called Sprints which range between 1 to 4 weeks. At the end of the Sprint, a small increment of the product is delivered to the customer. This increment should add value to the customer and of high quality and user should be able to use it if they decide to us it. So, product increment should be fully developed and tested and usable addition to the product.

On the first day of the sprint, Development team and PO get together for a meeting called Sprint Planning to decide how much from Product Backlog should be taken into Sprint based on Development Team's capacity and capability. This work is called Sprint Backlog. Once the Sprint is planned, the Development Team works collaboratively every day. The development team meets at least once a day for a 15-minute synch up called Daily Scrum to make sure that they are all on the same page. They identify any impediments that cause the Sprint goal to fail. ScrumMaster helps the team and PO in resolving those impediments so that they go forward.

The goal for the team to deliver a working Product Increment at the end of the sprint. Once the Product Increment is created, PO invites few stakeholders to review the product and give their feedback. The development team demonstrates what they have produced in the Sprint in a meeting called Sprint Review. Based on the feedback, the product will be adjusted if needed.

The Development Team and PO meet to reflect on what went well and what could be better after the Sprint Review in a meeting called Sprint Retrospective to identify any improvement areas they can work on. Product Owner and Development team meets few times every sprint to look at the Product Backlog to make it ready for the upcoming sprints. These activities are called Product Backlog Refinement. Since Product Backlog should be kept evolving to allow changes for the product, the product Backlog Refinement is an on going process to make the elaborate the requirement just in time.

Scrum Master helps Product Owner and Development team by Facilitating Scrum meetings effectively, coaching them on the Scrum Values and Process.

Success of Scrum implementation heavily depends on Scrum Master role. This is not an authoritative role. Scrum Master is like a Servant Leader who serves the team and help them achieve the goals. For Scrum Master to be effective, the role should be empowered i.e Scrum Master should be given full authority to implement Scrum Process. Other than understanding Scrum Framework in depth, Scrum Master needs to acquire few additional skills like Facilitation, Coaching, Mentoring, Teaching to effectively guide the Scrum Team.

1.1.23. What are the five phases of risk management?

1. Risk identification
2. Risk categorization
3. Risk response
4. Risk review
5. Risk closure

1.1.24. What are the main tools used in a Scrum project?

- JIRA

- Rally

- Version One

- Azure

1.1.25. How can a Scrum Master track the progress of a Sprint?

Scrum Masters can track the Sprint progress by using the Sprint burndown chart. The vertical axis shows the new estimate of work remaining while the horizontal one shows the number of Sprints.

This graph shows, each day, a new estimate of how much work remains until the Team is finished.

Product Backlog Item	Sprint Task	Volunteer	Initial Estimate of Effort	New Estimates of Effort Remaining at end of Day...					
				1	2	3	4	5	6
	modify database	Sanjay	5	4	3	0	0	0	
As a buyer, I want to place a book in a shopping cart	create webpage (UI)	Jing	3	3	3	2	0	0	
	create webpage (Javascript logic)	Tracy & Sam	2	2	2	2	2	0	
	write automated acceptance tests	Sarah	5	5	5	5	5	0	
	update buyer help webpage	Sanjay & Jing	3	3	3	3	3	0	
	. . .								
Improve transaction processing performance	merge DCP code and complete layer-level tests		5	5	5	5	5	5	
	complete machine order for pRank		3	3	8	8	8	8	
	change DCP and reader to use pRank http API		5	5	5	5	5	5	
. . .		. . .	. . .						
		Total	50	49	48	44	43	34	

Figure 1.7: Tracking Progress during Sprint – Example 1

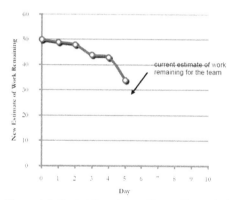

Figure 1.8: Sprint Burndown Chart – Example 1

Task	Task Owner	Hours of Work Remaining on Each Day of the Sprint									
		Day 1	Day 2	Day 3	Day 4	Day 5	Day 6	Day 7	Day 8	Day 9	Day 10
Configure database and space IDs for Trac	Sanjay	4	4	3	1	0					
Use test data to tune the learning and action model	Jing	2	2	2	2	1					
Setup a cart server code to run as apache server	Philip	3	3	5	2	0					
Implement pre-Login Handler	Tracy	3	3	3	3	3					
Merge DCP code and complete layer-level tests	Jing	5	5	2	2	2					
Complete machine order for pRank	Jing	4	4	3	3	3					
Change DCP and reader to use pRank http API	Tracy	3	3	0	0	0					
Total		50	48	44	43	34					

Figure 1.9: Tracking Progress during Sprint – Example 2

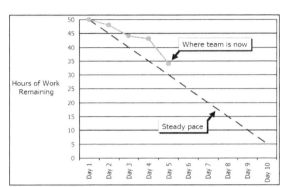

Figure 1.10: Sprint Burndown Chart – Example 2

1.1.26. What is timeboxing in Scrum?

Timeboxing means allotting a fixed unit of time for an activity. The unit of time is called a *time box*. The maximum length of a time box should be 15 minutes.

1.1.27. Is cancelling a Sprint possible? Who can cancel a Sprint?

A Sprint can be cancelled before the Sprint timebox limit ends. Only the Product Owner can cancel the sprint.

1.1.28. How is estimation in a Scrum project done? What are the techniques used for estimation?

Estimation in a Scrum project is done using relative Agile estimation techniques:

a. The T-shirt estimation technique
b. The planning poker estimation technique
c. The estimation by analogy technique
d. The disaggregation estimation technique

1.1.29. What are the roles involved in the Scrum framework?

A Scrum framework has three roles:

a. Scrum Master
b. Product Owner
c. Development team

1.1.30. What is the difference between change management in a Waterfall and in an Agile Scrum?

In Waterfall, change management is based on the change management plan, the change tracker and the release plan based on which the consultants deliver their work.

In agile there is no change management plan. Based on definition of ready product backlog, team is grooming Sprint backlog and delivering their work.

1.1.31. What is the purpose of a daily Scrum?

The daily Scrum meeting is for the team. It helps them self-organize towards their sprint commitment and set the context for the next day's work.

Daily SCRUM Meeting

Who Attends?	Development Team participation is mandatory. Product Owner or SCRUM Master participation is optional. But they can attend it based on the request.
When Happens?	Every day of the Sprint. **Choose a time that works for everyone.** It is held at the same time and place every day to reduce complexity.
Time-box	Maximum length of 15 minutes or less.
Input	Sprint Goal and Sprint Backlog
Outcome	Plan for next 24 hours and List of impediments (if any).
General Questions discussed	During the meeting, each Team member explains: <ul><li>What did he do yesterday that helped the team meet the Sprint Goal?</li><li>What will he do today to help the team meet the Sprint Goal?</li><li>Does he see any impediments that prevent him or the team from meeting the Sprint Goal?</li></ul> In a nutshell, it's interactive bilateral communication to understand: <ul><li>Where the Development Team is in terms of achieving Sprint Goal?</li><li>How Development Team can do differently, i.e., how Development Team can change the tactics to</li></ul>

	achieve more towards Sprint Goal in order to produce releasable product increment? • Development team tracks sprint roadmap progress based on Sprint Burndown / Burn up Charts where Effort **Unit Story Points** is plotted against Sprint number of day.
Generic Challenges	- The team is all working on separate things, no common Sprint Goal. - 'Mini-waterfall' syndrome i.e., cross dependency. - Self-organisation is a buzz word that has little practical meaning for the team. - All Teams are not in sync in case of distributed teams. - Mobile Friendly Cloud enabled cost optimum tool is missing for 24/7/365 customer support. - JIRA Tool has many limitations.
Daily Scrum Meeting Best Practices	• Choose a time that works for everyone. • Always focus on outcome rather than output. • Always focus on achieving Sprint Goal. • Keep stand-up efficient and keep everyone engaged, avoid making duplicate conversation and make the discussion short and crispy. Rotate who keeps time to make sure everyone is accountable and invested. If everything is fine, you may make it less than 15 minutes. Remember it's a problem identification meeting, but it is not problem solving meeting. • Stand in a *circle* near your desks. • Review and update sprint backlog every day. • No side conversations. • Meeting rules notice. • Same time and same place every day. Make effective use of **Daily Scrum Meeting (DSM) Tool**, JIRA Tool, Stride + stand-up for distributed teams. **DSM)**APPLICATION SOLVES MANY

	PRACTICAL ISSUES THAT EVERY PROJECT EXPERIENCES IN THE DEVELOPMENT STAGE. Manage your workload, communicate with your team, and celebrate success.
Benefits of Daily Scrum Meeting	<ul><li>Improves communication within the Team.</li><li>Identifies impediments, if any, in order to facilitate an early removal of the same, so as to minimize impact on the Sprint.</li><li>Highlights and promote quick decision-making.</li><li>Improves the team's level of knowledge.</li></ul>
Tools / techniques used	DSM Tool , JIRA Tool, Stride + stand-up for distributed teams. Telemetry technique is used to measure value. Dot Voting and Bottom-Up facilitation techniques are used for decision making.
Summary	Update and coordination by continuous inspection and adaptation of the sprint backlog, it's a planning event, not status tracking events.

1.1.32. What do you understand by the term scope creep? How do you prevent it from happening?

If the requirements are not properly defined at the start and new features are added to the product already being built, a scope creep occurs. To prevent it:

1. The requirements must be clearly specified.
2. The project progress must be monitored.
3. Effective grooming of sprint backlog must be done.

1.1.33. What are the most common risks in a Scrum project?

1. A scope creep
2. Timeline issues
3. Budget issues

1.1.34. What do you understand by Minimum Viable Product in Scrum?

A **Minimum Viable Product** (**MVP**) is a product with the minimum required features to be shown to the stakeholders and be eligible to ship for production.

1.1.35. What is the major advantage of using Scrum?

Early feedback, as well as the production of the Minimal Viable Product to the stakeholders, would be the main advantages of using it.

1.1.36. What does DoD mean? How can this be achieved?

Definition of Done is formed by a list of tasks that define the work's quality. It is used to decide whether an activity from the Sprint backlog is completed.

General
- Create the feature branch and push the changes according to above recommendations
- Code produced (all 'to do' items in code completed)
- Code commented, checked in and run against current version in source control
- Peer reviewed (or produced with pair programming) and meeting development standards
- Builds without errors - check Sonar
- Unit tests written and passing
- Deployed to system test environment and passed system tests
- Passed **User Acceptance Testing (UAT)** and signed off as meeting requirements
- Any build/deployment/configuration changes implemented/documented/communicated
- Relevant documentation/diagrams produced and/or updated
- Remaining hours for task set to zero and task closed

AEM
- Component name are the same in the codebase and in the dialog
- TouchUI dialog is defined for the component
- Component lifecycle (add component, edit dialog, activate for publish) is tested:
  - I. Default-values are implemented where necessary and tested.
  - II. Component is tested in the targeted browsers.
  - III. Changing component properties should not break the current and other components.
- Sonar test passed by Java code
- Test coverage level is covered
- Component / feature has been tested on publish instance (with a dispatcher)
- Sample content for the component has been added
- Clients for the component has been updated with css and js files

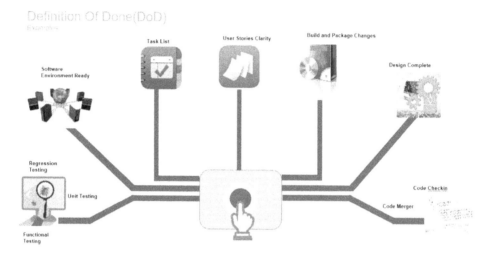

Figure 1.11: Definition Of Done – Example 1

Sample Definition of Done
- Code produced (all 'to do' items in code completed)
- Code commented, checked in and run against current version in source control
- Peer reviewed (or produced with pair programming) and meeting development standards
- Builds without errors
- Unit tests written and passing
- Deployed to system test environment and passed system tests
- Passed **User Acceptance Testing** (**UAT**) and signed off as meeting requirements
- Any build / deployment / configuration changes are implemented / documented / communicated
- Relevant documentation / diagrams produced and / or updated
- Remaining hours for task set to zero and task closed

Definition of Done

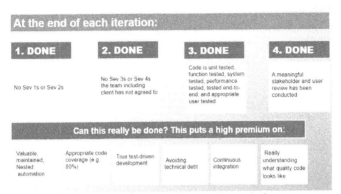

Figure 1.12: Definition Of Done – Example 2

1.1.37. What is velocity in Scrum?

Velocity calculates the total effort the team has put into a Sprint. The number is obtained by adding all the story points from the previous Sprint. It is a guideline for the team to understand the number of stories they can do in a Sprint.

1.1.38. List out the disadvantages of Scrum

- Daily Scrum meetings require frequent reviews and substantial resources.

- A successful project relies on the maturity and dedication of the whole team.

- The uncertainty of the product, the changes, and frequent product delivery remain present during the Scrum cycle.

- It depends on a significant change.

1.1.39. Scrum phases and processes

Scrum Phases and Processes

Initiate	Plan & Estimate	Implement	Review & Retrospect	Release
Create Project Vision	Create User Stories	Create Deliverables	Demonstrate and Validate Sprint	Ship Deliverables
Identify Scrum Master & Stakeholder(s)	Estimate User Stories	Conduct Daily Standup	Retrospect Sprint	Retrospect Project
Form Scrum Team	Commit User Stories	Groom Prioritized Product Backlog		
Develop Epics	Identify Tasks			
Create Prioritized Product Backlog	Estimate Tasks			
Conduct Release Planning	Create Sprint Backlog			

Figure 1.13: SCRUM phases and processes in a nutshell

1.1.40. SCRUM Flow

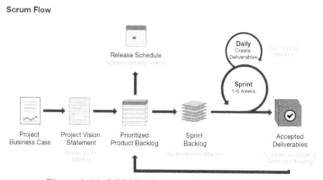

Figure 1.14: SCRUM Process Flow in a nutshell

1.1.41. Definition of Ready

Having a **Definition of Ready** means that stories must be immediately actionable.

Sample Definition of Ready
- User Story is clear
- User Story is testable

- User Story is feasible
- User Story defined
- User Story Acceptance Criteria defined
- User Story dependencies identified
- User Story sized by development team
- Scrum Team accepts user experience artefacts
- Performance criteria identified, where appropriate
- Scalability criteria identified, where appropriate
- Security criteria identified, where appropriate
- Person who will accept the User Story is identified
- Team has a good idea what it will mean to Demo the User Story

1.1.42. PDCA Cycle in SCRUM

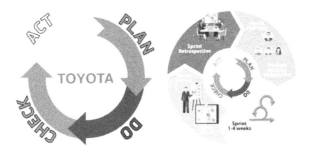

Figure 1.15: PDCA cycle in SCRUM

1.1.43. Why SCRUM Master is a Servant Leader?

SCRUM Master is system thinker. He / she has more value to:

a. Empathy

b. Active listening

c. Persuasion

d. Conflict resolution

e. Effective questioning skills

f. Grooming others

g. Self-awareness

h. Continuous learning

i. Credibility

1.1.44. What factor decides you whether you will do Project in SCRUM way?

When in complex environment we have specified timebox and definition of ready in Product backlog for our development work, i.e., where volume of work is predictable we can use SCRUM.

1.1.45. SCRUM real life issue

Suppose, tomorrow, two SCRUM team members took sick leave. You are supposed to give delivery after two weeks. You are following waterfall methodology. What you should do? All other team members are very busy and primary (P1) and secondary resource (P2) concept is not there.

We will check from the resource that whether anybody is doing any low priority work where delivery date is far later. So, we will ask them to do High priority work. We will ask them to keep aside the low priority work.

1.1.46. What did you do as SCRUM Master to prevent scope creep?

Where agile methods (like scrum) in itself will reduce the risk of scope creep through iterations as well as refinement of user stories only for the relevant sprint, i.e., effectively grooming sprint backlog from definition of ready Product backlog, the issues may still apply within the shorter lifecycles. Hence, scope management is still necessary and the principles are still applicable.

1.1.47. Example of one positive risk in your SCRUM project

We are finishing second sprint well ahead of delivery schedule.

1.1.48. Example of one negative risk in your SCRUM project

The product owner on the project quitting the job, even if his backup is not ready.

1.1.49. What are the main reasons for crashing schedule in your SCRUM project?

Delivering products well ahead of project milestone date.

1.1.50. Can we use DevOps in your SAP scrum project?

Yes,

By using ABAPGIT and Jenkins as per latest update from SAP TechEd.

1.1.51. In SCRUM, where customers are involved?

In sprint review and in sprint planning, customers are involved.

1.1.52. What makes daily SCRUM a waste of time?

a. The team members are doing multi-tasking. They are not in sync with each other's. They put more stress on individual performance. They put less importance on team work.
b. The team members are working on SCRUMBUT project. It is not 100% Scrum. It is not 100% waterfall.
c. The team members are geographically distributed in multiple countries. Each team member is not aware of other's work. They put less importance on self-organized team.

1.1.53. What techniques are used in daily SCRUM?

Dot voting and bottom up facilitation techniques are used for decision making.

1.1.54. Who attends daily SCRUM?

- Development team participation is mandatory.

- Product owner or scrum master participation is optional.

1.1.55. What are the differences between Product backlog and Sprint backlog?

Product Backlog	Sprint Backlog
• The Requirements	• Individuals signs up for work of their own choosing
• A list of all desired work on the project	• Estimated work remaining is updated daily
• Ideally expressed such that each item has value to the users or customers of the product	• Any team member can add, delete, change the Sprint backlog
• Prioritized by the Product owner (MoSCoW rule)	• If work is unclear, define a sprint backlog item with a larger amount of time and break it down later
• Reprioritized at the start of each Sprint	• Update work remaining as more becomes known

1.1.56. MoSCoW Prioritization technique

Letter	Stands for	Which means
M	Must Have	• Minimum set of essential requirements, without which the system would be useless (MMF) • All of these requirements must be satisfied.
S	Should Have	• Important requirements for which there is a short-term work-around. The system is useful without them. • These requirements can be included in the initial project scope, but may be removed from the project scope to accommodate changed

		requirements.
C	Could Have	• These requirements are valuable and nice-to-have, but can easily be left out of the solution. • These requirements may be left out of the initial scope of the release in order to accommodate a time constraint.
W	Would have/Won't have	• Time-permitting. • As changes to requirements or project progress dictates, lower priority requirements may be removed from the scope of the project.

1.1.57. Scrum master certification exam sample questions

You need to attend two days' workshop to have idea on scrum master certification questions.

1.1.58. Is it difficult to crack a Scrum Master interview?

No. You need to have atleast two years of hands-on scrum experience.

1.1.59. What are the primary skills that a recruiter looks into?

Servant leadership

1.1.60. Latest updates for interviewees

From Agile scrum blogs you can get it.

1.1.61. Important tips to prepare for an interview

1. Review the most commonly asked questions, listed above.
2. Do some previous research on the company.
3. Find a way to develop a connection with the interviewer.
4. Be positive and be confident.
5. End the interview on a positive note.

Conclusion

Now that the Scrum Master's profession is in such demand, this career ranks 10th on the list of the most promising jobs. A professional Scrum Master salary ranges from $107,280 to $136,748 per annum. Having a certification adds value to an applicant's résumé.

There are many questions during an interview that do not have a right or wrong answer. It all depends on each organization and the applicant's perspective when resolving the situation. Hence, one should also be prepared for general questions.

Meta description: Preparing to clear your Scrum interview? Here's the article that exposes you to 100 PLUS most commonly asked Scrum Master interview questions and the best answers.

1.1.62. Common Agile Product Development Myths

Introduction: Agile began as an iterative, collaborative, value-driven approach to developing software.
It was originally conceived as a framework to help structure work on complex projects with dynamic, unpredictable characteristics.
But since then, it has evolved into somewhat of a philosophy or world view, with a set of well-articulated values and principles common between Agile's many varieties.

But we have noticed that many times people are misinterpreting some concepts in Agile. We can discuss all here so the next time you are going to start a project and want to use Agile and Scrum, step back and analyze the scenario. Ask yourself about the best fit for the project and make sure you don't fall into these traps of Myths.

All the best!

Myth	Reality
❖ **Agile is used only for Software development.**	✓ **This is entirely false.** ✓ Agile works for **all kinds of Products** development, (example, Toyota cars, HP Laptops etc.), software is one amongst them. ✓ Agile these days is used for all forms of product development, from **physical products to cloud-based software-as-a-service (SaaS).** ✓ But beyond product development (**both hardware and software**), agile is being used successfully by: ➤ Marketing teams to plan and execute campaigns ➤ Lawyers to manage cases and workload ➤ Students planning exams ➤ Couples planning weddings ➤ Families for improving time together ➤ Human resources to manage their workload ➤ Organizational transformation efforts, in particular when transitioning to agile ➤ Senior leadership teams to manage their organizations ➤ And, of course, many more.

Myth	Reality
❖ Stakeholders can introduce change whenever they want.	✓ **Not True always.** ✓ If the change is introduced at the right time, there may be little or no cost. Introduced at the wrong time, though, and there is a cost. ✓ Being agile cannot eliminate all costs of stakeholders introducing change. However, good agile teams can reduce the cost of change regardless of when the change is introduced. Common ways of doing this are as follows: • short iterations • small product backlog items • Finishing each product backlog item as quickly as possible, usually by minimizing the number of items being worked on concurrently. ✓ None of this is to say that teams shouldn't welcome appropriate changes. Some stakeholder-requested changes can be very important. But, **the benefit of making each change needs to be assessed against the cost of changing and that cost is not always zero.**

Myth	Reality
❖ Everyone needs to be a generalist on an Agile team	✓ **This is entirely false.** ✓ Agile teams don't need everyone to have every skill. Instead, what agile teams need is to **value any individuals who do possess skills in multiple disciplines.** They can help each other always.(Example, dev team and testing team) ✓ Having a **few team members with multiple skills helps manage the balance of types of work.** That is, sometimes **the team needs more testing capacity.** ✓ But this can be accomplished on most teams even if a few team members are truly specialists and expert at only one discipline.

Myth	Reality
❖ Agile teams don't (or can't) plan.	✓ This is entirely false. ✓ Agile teams **don't have an upfront planning phase**. They **plan incrementally by continuous inspection and adaptation** based on Customer priority / business outcome. ✓ Instead, **good agile teams conduct planning as a series of smaller, recurring activities** that ensure their plans **always reflect the realities of the current situation.** ✓ In this way, teams develop **plans** the same way they develop products: by **inspecting and adapting.** ✓ Consider a traditional team with analysis, design, coding and testing phases. If lucky, that team may delay committing to a plan until the end of the design phase. But at that point, this team has no idea how fast they are at coding and testing—they haven't done any of those activities yet. ✓ In contrast, an agile team turns the entire build into multiple iterations. Each iteration includes a little analysis, design, coding, and testing. This gives the agile team more and earlier insight into how quickly it can turn ideas into new features.

Planning Process

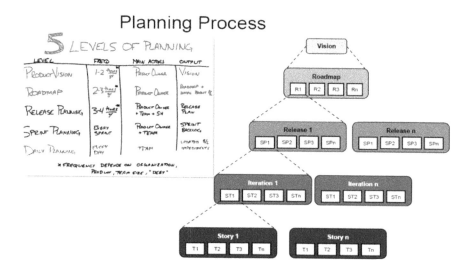

Figure 1.16: 5 Levels of Planning

Myth	Reality
❖ Agile teams create products with no architectural plan	✓ **This is entirely false.**
	✓ Agile teams **don't have an upfront phase** during which all architectural decisions are made. Instead the **architecture of a product emerges over time.**
	✓ They architect and design incrementally by continuous inspection and adaptation **based on Customer priority / business outcome.**
	✓ This occurs by **technical team members focusing first on any aspects of a product they consider risky.** For example, if delivering a product with the needed throughput will be challenging, the team and product owner would elect to work on functionality early on that reduces that risk.
	✓ In this way, the emergent architecture of an agile product is also intentional. The architecture doesn't just show up one day. It emerges gradually and guided by the intent of the technical team members.
	✓ This means that agile products do possess an underlying architecture. But decisions about that architecture are made as needed through the course of the project rather than being made entirely at the start of the project.

1.1.63. Three Types of "Scrum Teams"

Type 1: Groups that try to do Scrum
Most Dangerous

- Low-level of task interdependence.
- Do not need to work together as a team (Context does not require teamwork).
- Forced to do Scrum because that is what everyone else is doing.
- Group members hate Scrum because it does not work. How could it?
- Retrospectives add little to no value—Take seven random people in a bar and have them conduct a retrospective on the work they did not do together.

Vital Flaw: Thinking that method precedes context.

Sports analogy: Wrestlers

Type 2: Scrum "Teams"

Characteristics

- People who have a high-level of task interdependence but do not know how to work together as a team.
- They do Scrum things and worry about buffer, writing user stories, and happiness metrics.
- Think sending an email builds situational awareness and is part of closed-loop communication.
- Spend time talking about the differences between themes, initiatives, epics, and stories.
- Retrospectives change frequently and tend to focus on what went well, what didn't, and so on.

- Planning sessions and the daily Scrum look nothing alike.
- Members and coaches hold several certifications and use phrases such as: *That's not agile* and *Let's self-organize and move these chairs toward the wall so we can…*
- Lacks agility but claim they are agile.
- Managers in the organization consider the team to be *Agile* because they are either (1) trained in Scrum or (2) are doing Scrum.
- Have a *me* attitude.
- Low-level of employee engagement.
- May occasionally achieve a 2X improvement in velocity.

Vital Flaw: Assumption that people with high-technical skills or advanced education know how to team.

Sports Analogy: 2002-2004 USA Men's Basketball Dream Team (**Hint**: they lost to teams that knew how to play together)

Type 3: Teams that use Scrum
Significant Competitive Advantage

Characteristics

- Two or more people who work interdependently, adaptively, and dynamically towards a shared and valued goal/objective/mission (This is actually the definition of a team)
- Improve team interactions daily
- Know how to mitigate cognitive biases
- Each member can lead any event
- Members display fallibility
- Prioritized Teamwork training over Framework training (Scrum)
- Practice closed-loop communication
- Challenge each other's assumptions
- Detect weak signals
- Have a *we* attitude
- Scrum used to help prioritize work, build a cadence, and create a container
- Scrum is a force multiplier
- Teams know how to separate decisions from outcomes
- Follow the 60/40 rule in retrospectives: 60% focus on teamwork (Teaming skills) and 40% on task work
- Not uncommon to see a 4X to 16X improvement in velocity

Vital Flaw: Waiting! Waiting is failure!

Sports Analogy: All Blacks, New England Patriots, 1980 USA Men's Olympic Hockey Team.

Bottom line: If you want to create agility, prioritize Teamwork over Frameworks.
Give more stress on team outcome achieved rather than efforts spent.

1.1.64. Agile Budget Management

Agile budget calculation is very hot buzzword now. Here, you need to calculate your labor costs, non-labor costs, NFR costs apart from calculating your labor costs for functional/technical requirements.

How is your budget being allocated today?

• Top down decision by leader/leaders

• Same budget as last year with small changes

• Start from scratch each year aligning resources to priorities

• I don't know

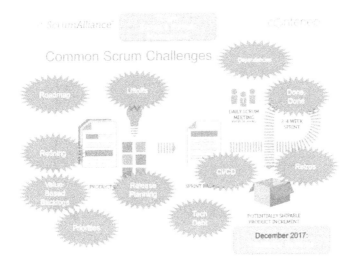

Figure 1.17: SCRUM – Common challenges

Image source: https://www.scrumalliance.org

In Agile we are getting big business requirements in terms of Epics which are combination of many related user stories.

- Prepare and estimate the project requirements using planning oker
- Determine the team's velocity

Prepare and estimate the project requirements using planning poker

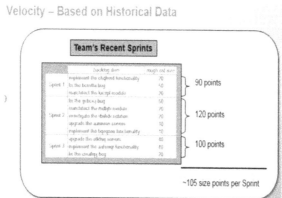

Figure 1.18: Calculation of Velocity per Sprint - Example

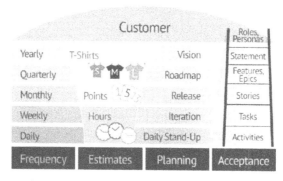

Figure 1.19: Different types of planning in SCRUM

Image source: https://www.scrumalliance.org

Reference – Go to the following URL to have detailed case study.

https://www.linkedin.com/pulse/agile-budget-calculation-utopia-worldwide-across/

1.1.65. Agile Contract Management

Time and Material (T&M) type contracts are a good fit for Agile engagements.

Fixed Price / Fixed Capacity (FPFC) contract is most suitable for Agile whereas a contract with Fixed Price / Fixed scope must be avoided.

We have noticed that most clients know only a small percentage of their complete requirements at the start of any new project. This is more so for an application / site development and we observed something very similar in platform / technology migration situations as well. Later, most customers wanted to add new features as well which makes it somewhat like a new development. Asking them to define the priorities is almost impossible. What we have tried here are various things (in case of fixed price).

For risk & Impact / analyse and design phase we have put T&M contract, for Build & testing till UAT we have put *Fixed Price – 70/30 mode* which puts 30% of the revenue on a penalty mode if there is any slippage in timeline or quality. Closely work with client to create contract – defining the prerequisites and exit criteria. After UAT till Go-Live and support / hypercare phase we have put T&M contract.

Reference – Go to the below URL to have detailed case study.

https://www.linkedin.com/pulse/agile-scrum-contract-best-practices-sudipta-malakar-csp/

1. We try and explain that any changes to the requirements will swap out an equal sized but lower priority requirement. Thus the client keeps the budget in check and has the flexibility even late in the project life cycle to add / remove requirements.

2. We try and have a T & M requirement phase where the Product Backlog is frozen (maybe 80%) and then give a fixed bid quote (with appropriate assumptions and margins for error).

3. We have clauses in the contract where we say that project estimates will be revisited at specified intervals and all estimations etc. will be transparent.

While these measures have helped, it really depends a lot on the client's understanding of Agile and willingness to collaborate. Otherwise it's always a tough and bumpy ride, especially in Agile projects.

Figure 1.20: Different types of Agile Contracts
Image Source: PMI PMBOK

Other popular contract types include paying by features contract, time and materials contract, fixed price and fixed scope contract, and fixed profit contract.

Thorup and Jensen (2009) explain in their paper the option of Graduated Fixed Price (see Exhibit3)

Project Completion	Total Fee	Graduated Rate
Finish Early	$87,000	$117/hour
Finish On-Time	$100,000	$100/hour
Finish Late	$113,000	$90/hour

Figure 1.21: Contract - Illustration
Image Source: PMI PMBOK

1.1.66. Agile – Key Takeaways

By agile, we mean a number of things:

- Enhanced flexibility
- Empowering employees to work where, when and how they choose
- Iterative delivery of projects
- Co-ownership of projects with the client / customer
- The opportunity to adapt ways of working and processes as objectives change and move on throughout a project lifecycle.

Which of these descriptions best applies to the project management function within the organization?

- Established processes in place, with ongoing improvements and innovations introduced, based on feedback from monitoring and evaluation.

Senior managers are actively keen that the **Portfolio Program Manager (PPM)** function becomes more strategic (e.g. has more tangible and identifiable impact on overall business goals and finances).

Agile is a value driven approach, not plan driven.

A plan driven, project focused, approach is what we learned when we got our PMP's. Everything is planned up front. Requirements are fixed, and cost and schedule are estimated. We then report status based on how the project is doing compared to the plan.

When it comes to software development, we know a plan driven approach is flawed. Yet, many companies continue to use it. Why? Why do we punish project teams for being over budget or behind schedule when we know it's the process that's broken?

We need to shift our mindset from project focus, to product focus.

Product focus is a value driven, adaptive process. It doesn't punish teams for change. It anticipates change and even welcomes it.

In a value driven approach, cost is fixed, and features are estimated. It's the reverse of a plan driven approach. Investment is made at the product level, not a project level. People are dedicated to teams, and the teams stay intact.

It's not for small tech firms only. Target, for example, has completely shifted to a product focus model. They get it, and they're not alone. Many large companies are organizing cross functional teams around products. They are bringing IT and business people together to focus on delivering business outcomes.

If your company is going Agile, ask yourself, are you ready to move on from traditional project management? Are you ready to no longer have a PMO? Are you ready to change? If yes, then it's time to embrace a product focused mindset. If no, then continue using waterfall, but don't call it Agile.

Bottom line: If you want to create agility, prioritize Teamwork over Frameworks.

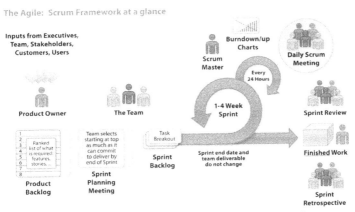

Figure 1.22: Agile SCRUM Process flow in a nutshell

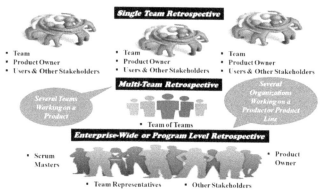

Figure 1.23: SCRUM Retrospective types

1.1.67. Agile – Where following Agile is not appropriate

Agile is not appropriate for...

- PROJECTS without significant complexity, urgency and uniqueness.

- TEAMS which are not self-organizing and do not believe in inspecting and adapting.

- ORGANISATIONS which do not invest in good XP practices (e.g. TDD, CI etc.) and cross-functional teams.

- CUSTOMERS who are not willing to be part of the product development team and provide continuous feedback.

- Big Bang – across the board changes without experimentation

- Iterative development without Automated Tests

- Sprints (Iterations) that deliver incomplete work

- Doing mini-waterfalls within the Sprint (Iterations)

- Implementing Agile without believing in its core Values and Principles.

- Projects where scope is almost frozen and doing upfront planning / design

- Projects just "DOING AGILE" rather than "BEING AGILE" mindset

- Projects believing in doing all Customer Projects using 100% automation and following analogous estimation

- Projects using PUSH principles rather than following PULL principles

1.1.68. On what parameters Sprints are empirical?

Sprints are empirical in regards to:

- ✓ Outcomes (how valuable will this feature be?)
- ✓ Outputs (how much can we get done?)
- ✓ Approaches (how should we work?)

1.1.69. Mention some major Product Owner anti-patterns.

Product Owner Anti-Patterns
In pairs or small groups discuss your experience with the following anti-patterns or speculate on the impact of:

• Absent Product Owner
• Product Owner ScrumMaster
• Token Product Owner
• Penniless Product Owner

1.1.70. Mention the approach user need to follow in order to achieve outcome of "Agile Manifesto Results Pyramid"?

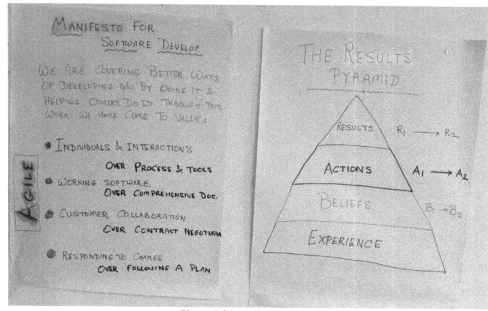

Figure 1.24: Agile Manifesto

Try to follow Bottom-up approach in "The Results Pyramid" to achieve outcome.

1.1.71. What is your current role/function relating to Agile Way of Working?

- Scrum Master
- Product Owner
- Agile Manager
- Agile Coach
- Other

1.1.72. What meeting do you find most valuable within the Agile Way of Work?
- Refinement
- Planning meeting
- Daily Stand-up
- Review meeting
- Retrospective meeting
- Other

1.1.73. How important would you rank the Retrospective meeting? (from never till always)

- o 1
- o 2
- o 3
- o 4
- o 5

1.1.74. When attending a Retrospective meeting, do you (sometimes) facilitate and/or participate the process?

- o Participate
- o Facilitate and Participate
- o Facilitate

1.1.75. Did you do any formal training on facilitation?

- o No
- o Yes

1.1.76. Which training did you follow for facilitation?

1.1.77. I think facilitating the process is:

- o Very easy
- o Easy
- o Somewhat challenging
- o Challenging
- o Very difficult

1.1.78. What in particular do you find challenging/difficult?

1.1.79. When we have a retrospective, we follow the 5-step process from Esther Derby and Diana Larsen: (Setting the Stage, Gather Data, Generate Insights, Decide What to Do, Close the Retrospective)

- o Yes
- o No
- o I don't know

1.1.80. When we have our retrospective all team members are present (including Product Owner and Scrum Master).

- o always
- o often
- o mostly
- o sometimes

o never

1.1.81. When we have team members not participating in our retro it is usually for the following reasons?

- o they are needed on more urgent work
- o they have other meetings which are more important
- o they think they don't need to be there
- o it is their regular day off
- o they were not aware of the meeting
- o they don't see the need for such a meeting (only when chosen openly and not by some of the other anti-patterns mentioned)

1.1.82. What other reason can you mention when team members not participating in the team retrospective?

1.1.83. We allocate the appropriate amount of time for our retrospective, 3 hours for a monthly sprint, 1.5 hours for a two-weekly sprint or a proportional equivalent for other timeboxes).

- o always
- o often
- o mostly
- o sometimes
- o never

1.1.84. Our retrospective is finished within the given timeframe.

- o always
- o often
- o mostly
- o sometimes
- o never

1.1.85. For our retrospectives the team members arrive on time or earlier.

- o always
- o often
- o mostly
- o sometimes
- o never

1.1.86. Cancelling our retrospective is what we do.

- o always
- o often
- o mostly

o sometimes
o never

1.1.87. Our retrospectives get postponed.

o always
o often
o mostly
o sometimes
o never

1.1.88. If our work in the Sprint is not yet ready, we use the time for the retrospective as a buffer.

o always
o often
o mostly
o sometimes
o never

1.1.89. In our retrospectives people listen to each another.

o always
o often
o mostly
o sometimes
o never

1.1.90. In our retrospectives people do interrupt others.

o always
o often
o mostly
o sometimes
o never

1.1.91. In our retrospectives subgroups and separate discussions emerge.

o always
o often
o mostly
o sometimes
o never

1.1.92. My team members understand and support the need for retrospectives.

o Yes
o No

1.1.93. In our retrospectives there is an atmosphere of trust and respect.
- ○ always
- ○ often
- ○ mostly
- ○ sometimes
- ○ never

1.1.94. We have a suitable location available for our retrospectives.
- ○ always
- ○ often
- ○ mostly
- ○ sometimes
- ○ never

1.1.95. We have a suitable location available for our retrospectives.
- ○ always
- ○ often
- ○ mostly
- ○ sometimes
- ○ never

1.1.96. The location has the right properties for a good retrospective (absence of obstructing tables, walls to be used, daylight etc.)
- ○ always
- ○ often
- ○ mostly
- ○ sometimes
- ○ never

1.1.97. All necessary equipment for a good retro such as flipcharts, whiteboards, markers, sticky notes, large posters and so on, are available.
- ○ always
- ○ often
- ○ mostly
- ○ sometimes
- ○ never

1.1.98. As a result of our retrospective we have a plan on what and how we want to improve.
- ○ always
- ○ often
- ○ mostly
- ○ sometimes
- ○ never

1.1.99. In our retrospective we inspect the improvement plan/items of our previous sprint.

- o always
- o often
- o mostly
- o sometimes
- o never

1.1.100. Our retrospectives are boring, we do the same things over and over again and have little or no variation.

- o Strongly Agree
- o Agree
- o Neutral
- o Disagree
- o Strongly Disagree

1.1.101. Within our retrospectives we act as a group of individuals and not as a team.

- o Strongly Agree
- o Agree
- o Neutral
- o Disagree
- o Strongly Disagree

1.1.102. Our retrospectives are not visited by managers.

- o Strongly Agree
- o Agree
- o Neutral
- o Disagree
- o Strongly Disagree

1.1.103. My team members feel retrospectives are mandatory. (from never till always)

- o 1
- o 2
- o 3
- o 4
- o 5.

1.1.104. Results from our retrospectives get unwanted shared with people outside the team. (from never till always)

- o 1
- o 2
- o 3
- o 4
- o 5

1.1.105. Our retro outcomes lack ownership, follow-up and SMART definition. (from never till always)
- o 1
- o 2
- o 3
- o 4
- o 5

1.1.106. Would you like to have a copy of the survey results?
- o Yes
- o No

1.1.107. Do you have other remarks or comments on the Retrospective event?
- o Yes
- o No

1.1.108. Roughly how many full-time employees currently work for your organization?
- o 1-10
- o 11-50
- o 51-200
- o 201-500
- o 501-1,000
- o 1,001-5,000
- o 5,001-10,000
- o 10,000+

1.1.109. What is your organization industry type?

1.1.110. Agile Contracts Nuts and Bolts
Introduction

The goal of agile contracts is to enable close cooperation between the project team and the business or the customer. This cooperation helps in redirecting team's efforts towards delivering value added features. This is also evident from the third value statement of the Agile Manifesto which states "Customer collaboration over contract negotiation". An agile approach requires more trust between the parties than a traditional approach, it focusses on what resources are trying to build, rather than bogging them down on debates about how changes will be negotiated of what the completion criteria really is.

An agile approach also requires the business to be more involved in providing feedback on iterations, reprioritization of the backlog and evaluating the value of change requests against the remaining work items. If there is a trust factor in place, agile contracts can be a great tool for extracting more value for the clients and thereby have a competitive advantage. However, when the trust factor is absent agile contracts will be a difficult buy in and may also not be suitable.

What is required to build an Agile contract?

The key element of building an agile contract is a mindset. To understand the type of mindset shift expected from different stakeholders, the below table can be useful: -

Stakeholder(s)	Traditional Mindset	Agile Mindset
Sales	Let's do whatever it takes to get the bid	Let's not focus just to get new customers, let's create happy ones too.
Procurement	We must know exactly what, when and how much and have a discount We want the cheapest price	There is a value in collaborative relationships and mutual motivation. We get what we pay for.
Legal	Let's reduce our risks and make sure if things go wrong, we don't suffer	Agile can lower the risk and there are existing models to support it.
Architects	Let's create the design upfront to meet our deadlines	Let's keep our design options open till the time it's feasible
Program Management	Let's reduce risk by having phase gate milestones to check the progress	Let's measure progress with working software, how much business value has been achieved and how much risk has reduced.

Principles of Agile Contracts

Principle	Focus On	Results in
Alignment of Incentives	Pay for outcomes, Not for Effort Responsive to changes Sharing Benefits of continuous Improvement	Encourage vendors to create value Have ability to update scope Have rewards for vendors demonstrating efficiency
Collaboration and Transparency	Maintaining Trust Focus on vision and not process	Assume parties act in good faith Clear goals/objectives in contract & reference backlog for detailed scope
Ability to Inspect and Adapt	Establish regular feedback cycles Set the rules of engagement But anticipate the unexpected	Specify Sprint cycle and review, retrospectives, and backlog refinement meetings Identify roles & processes to give feedback, refine backlog, accept work Define how likely extensions of initial contract will be handled

Some sample sections of a contract

Section	Example
Period of Performance	2-week sprints, until ended by either party
Engagement Resources	A Dev Team in the Philippines with a Scrum Master & Business Analyst A customer Product Owner to answer any questions
Scope of Work	Clear goals for first 3 sprints (proof of concept) After that, contract backlog will define scope
Client & Vendor Responsibilities	Client provides feedback & maintains prioritized backlog Vendor provides transparency and demo after every sprint
Fee Schedule	Vendor is paid at the end of each 1-week sprint
Termination/ Renewal	Both parties can decide to renew or cancel after each sprint review

Conclusion

No contract can make us agile but a bad contract will stop us from becoming agile and compromise the benefits from both parties to gain from agility.

1.1.111. Backlog Management in Agile

Product and solution requirements in various agile practices is managed through a list of prioritized requirements. This is of prioritized requirements is called backlog. Backlogs help in aligning the business priorities with priorities of engineering teams. A common backlog for a product ensures that the teams is always working on highest priority requirements which maximize the business value delivered by the team. So they help in creating a common focus for all the members of the development team.

Backlog gets refined and re-prioritized at different stages by stakeholders before development teams start working on it. At each of these stages as the backlog is refined, requirements can be identified more clearly. This may result in addition of more items to backlog. Additional requirements can also be identified based on team specific needs and they help the teams deliver more efficiently and with increased quality.

Depending on the stage of development or delivery and stakeholders, backlog can be of following 3 types –

> ➢ Portfolio Backlog
> ➢ Program Backlog
> ➢ Product Backlog

Portfolio Backlog

Portfolio backlog contains several Initiatives. These features are prioritized based on their business criticality relative to each other, vision of the organization and market trends. Some initiatives are also added to explore technical enhancements to support future development efforts. Any technical debt items to be worked on at the organizational level, are added to the list and relatively prioritized with other initiatives. As we learn more about changes in customer and market expectations, more initiatives can be added to the portfolio back and priorities need to be re-adjusted.

Portfolio backlog is maintained and updated by customer facing executives who have an understanding of organizations business, financial and technical context. They ensure that investment is aligned to business priorities of the organization and in-line with its vision.

In order to prioritize the initiatives, we need to understand the business value provided by them. Initiatives are prioritized relative to each other and sized at a high level (Small, Medium, Large, Extra Large etc.). If an initiative is too large or complex, other initiatives are added for studying it and bring clarity. This brings out dependencies and highlights the risks which would have been hidden otherwise.

There could be multiple initiatives on-going in the organization independently. Although it is desirable that these initiatives be completely independent, but since they are part of the same product or solution, there could be some dependencies among them. To create a valuable solution, it is important to understand these dependencies so that, a valuable solution/product for to customers can be created. Initiatives might need to be re-prioritized to create a solution, when we understand these dependencies. Business and Technical leaders responsible for these initiatives coordinate among themselves and prioritize the work to ensure that dependencies are taken care of.

Program Backlog

In order to accomplish the initiatives in portfolio, smaller and more manageable features are added in program backlog. Product management team is responsible for program backlog. With collaboration with customers, customer facing teams and engineering teams, product management adds features to program backlog. These features are prioritized based on the value delivered by them. If there are technical debts at program level, they are added to the backlog as well and prioritized along with features. Any significant architectural changes needed for upcoming features are prioritized as features in product backlog as well. Dependencies on features from other initiatives are also considered when prioritizing the features.

Program backlog refinement happens between two releases when feature development is in progress. Items in the program backlog need to be actively and continuously managed to align with market and customer needs. Priority and value created by features is assessed during interactions with customers, customer facing teams and product evangelists. Based on these interactions, new features are created and prioritized. If it is considered that lower priority features don't provide desired ROI, further development is stopped.

Any feature which is large, is broken down into smaller features such that each broken down feature can be completed within a release and creates value for the customer. Acceptance criteria for the features is added which determines when the feature is considered complete.

It is important to allocate time for technical debts and architectural features along with the customer features so that team can continue to develop customer at a sustainable pace. In order to have a balance between the three, a fixed proportion of each of these is agreed upon and capacity of the team is planned accordingly. Based on this assessment, a draft release content is formed. Release content is created for the subsequent 2 releases. It is then reviewed and adjusted based on new facts known at the start of the release in which it needs to be worked on.

Commitments for requirements planned for longer term is not considered as firm. Since the requirement is planned for a longer term, there is some uncertainty. Team might need to work on some other higher priority requirement than the one planned for log term. In such a case, it will be difficult for product management to manage the customer.

Product Backlog

Product backlog contains user stories required to build the feature in program backlog. It also contains user stories which team creates based on discussions and action items created in retrospective meeting. User stories related to technical debt, which enable the team to work more efficiently, are created and added to the product backlog as well.

Product Owner is responsible for creating and managing product backlog. SMEs and members of other leadership team negotiate with Product owner to add user stories related to technical debt and prioritized them. Based on the value these technical debt user stories will add and enhance the capability of the team, these user stories are prioritized along with user stories with create customer features. Product owner identifies the part product backlog which can be accomplished in a sprint and the business objective which would be met through it. Product owner also considers the capacity of the team when doing so.

During the sprint or development phase, development team allocates some time (max 10% according to Scrum guide) for grooming user stories for subsequent sprints. Feature is broken into more user stories and details are added to the new and existing ones. User stories are prioritized to deliver early business value to customer. User stories are estimated at a high level. User stories which are of higher priority have more details and clarity of scope and are ready to be taken-up in the upcoming 1-2 sprints. User stories which are of lower priority have less details. As more is learnt about the feature scope more details are added, or user stories are dropped, if they don't create the desired value.

If product development is using Scrum framework, during sprint planning, user stories are discussed, and team learns more about them. This discussion between team and product owner is important as team learns more about customer expectations through it. Based on this discussion, new user stories are identified, and details are added to them and previous user stories created by product owner initially. Based on the facts which have been uncovered in the sprint planning meeting, the team estimates the user stories again. Team takes-up high priority user stories for the sprint which they can complete and deliver value to customer. If user stories cannot be taken-up in the Sprint, they are sent back to the product backlog to be prioritized in the next Sprint.

Conclusion

Backlog gets refined at different staged by different people based on their area of expertise and exposure to product and customer they have. A common backlog keeps team and organization focused on a common goal. A summary of different types of backlogs and stakeholders responsible for them is as below –

Backlog type	Content	Stakeholder Responsible
Portfolio Backlog	Initiatives	Executives
Program Backlog	Features	Product Management
Product Backlog	User Stories	Product Owner

Backlogs are primarily focused on creating customer value. Some backlog items are added to experiment and get more clarity on features or approach to be taken for development. Backlog also contains some content which will help team become more efficient (technical debt related, action items from retrospective meeting etc.).

1.1.112. Agile Contracts - Modelling a transformation in contracting

Introduction to contracts:

Business dictionary definition of a 'Contract' is: A voluntary, deliberate, and legally binding agreement between two or more competent parties. A contractual relationship is evidenced by an offer, acceptance of the offer, and a valid (legal and valuable) consideration. Each party to a contract acquires rights and duties relative to the rights and duties of the other parties. However, while all parties may expect a fair benefit from the contract (otherwise courts may set it aside as inequitable) it does not follow that each party will benefit to an equal extent.

Any contract is defined by the level of risk each party involved is willing to accept. This involves three fundamental points to consider in contracting

1. "What is the cost/ budget?"
2. What is the duration / time estimate?
3. What are the deliverables/ scope?

Traditional contracts that were used in the industry are 1) Fixed-price contract where the payment amount does not depend on resources used or time expended 2) Time and material (T&M) contract in which billing clients happens for actual work scope based on hourly rates of labour. Customers are charged for the number of hours spent on a specific project, plus costs of materials consumed.

Amongst traditional ones, T&M contract is the most commonly used contract when comes to compatibility with agile methods where project scope is not yet fully known, and we have flexibility to modify the scope or vary the workloads as and when needed.

Capped T&M here there is cap on the price a customer needs to pay for the supplier is also a subset of T&M.

'Fixed' contracts are not suitable to agile but a reality as the trust level between parties are generally low.

Fixed contracts include 1) Fixed cost but flexible on scope and time,2) Fixed time but flexible on scope and time, 3) Fixed cost and time but flexible on scope 4) Fixed Cost and scope but flexible on time 5) Fixed time and scope but flexible on cost.

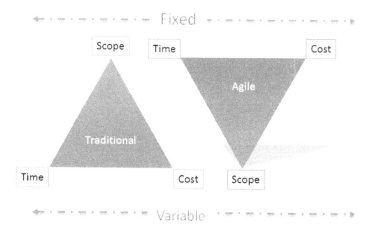

Figure 1.25: Triple constraints

Creating Agile contracts

When we think about agile contracts, we must consider agile manifesto statement "Customer collaboration over contract negotiation".

This essentially means that we must try and create a trust level between the parties involved in the contract to create collaboration which facilitate agility and a focus on outcomes rather than outputs.

Agile contracts are all incremental delivery contracts, which means that there is always a flexibility to both the parties to retrospect and part ways at regular prescribed points of time if the association is not making expected results.

Incremental means that they are as frequent as 2 weeks to 4 weeks as and when a team delivers to the customer.

If the relationship is new between both the parties and trust level is low, as in the pyramid of trust, we may start with fixed contracts.

Figure 1.26: Pyramid of Trust

Image reference: nngroup.com

Ideally, we may negotiate and start with a Fixed time and cost but flexible with scope contract for a Minimum Viable Product.

During the execution of the project, and incremental delivery retrospectives, both parties may move from baseline relevance to interest in each other and of preference over other suppliers.

MVP to product/ service development partnership takes few consistent ' Fixed time and cost but flexible with scope' associations bet weens two parties.

At this stage the trust level will be that of sharing personal and financial information between both parties under Non-disclosure agreements.

Moving to Outcome based Partnerships

True 'Trusted supplier', 'Outsource partner' tags require a supplier to start with 'routine' work and ' Focused' work contracts to prove the capability and resilience before starting out with ' Leverage' where both parties understand and work to their strengths. and finally, to strategic alliances.

Figure 1.27: Value Risk Matrix

Strategic and operational agility at both parties is an important factor for the success of any outcome-based partnerships. For example, both supplier and customer organizations may use Objectives and Key results (OKRs) in building operational sync and common measures of success of partnership in working - collaborating teams.

Outcome based contracting requires us to focus beyond output/deliverables to business outcome and creating win-win situations.

Figure 1.28: Traditional Contract vs. Outcome based Contract

'Rolls Royce - Power by hour' and 'GE aviation- True Choice Flight hour' are two good examples of Outcome based business contracts.

Challenges to Adoption of Outcome based model

Developing a common measurement and analysis system to agree on measures and metrics by both Service provider/Supplier and Customer is the primary challenge.

Second challenge is the mind set or cultural shift that is needed from both parties.

- Letting go of control of people and process to Supplier from customer.
- Both parties should be able to quantify risk of the engagement and move towards agreed common business goals.

Overcoming challenges

Set up a core team at leadership level facilitated by external executive coach/consultant to create a workshop for defining the rules of and boundaries of engagement would be a starting step.

Focus shall be on Transparency of business opportunities and challenges, Flexibility in choosing pricing models based on business situations and expected outcomes (refer risk model) and predictability of expected business outcomes and profits,

This includes defining both strategic and operational outcomes with common method of measurement i.e. KRA/KPIs at operational level.

Second step is to define OKRs at people at working level for working agreements.

Conclusion

Moving from Low trust competition to High Trust partnership and co-creation will need significant investment in transformation of leadership and workforce from a closed to open system thinking.

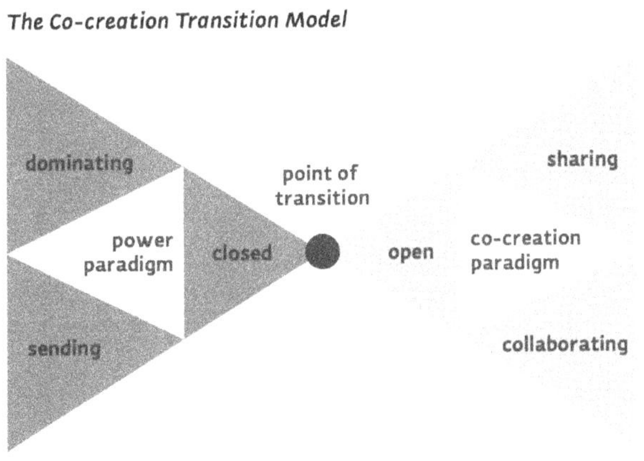

The Co-creation Transition Model

Figure 1.29: The Co-creation Transition Model

1.1.113. Role of Manager (People) in an Agile Organisation

In Agile Organizations, members are self-organized, empowered teams. They are constantly learning new skills from each other. A "Product Owner" prioritizing team's task, organizing and managing the Product Backlog. A "Scrum Master" removing impediments, escalating issues to ensure that team productivity and quality remains high. So, there is no specific role called project manager. *Are managers soon to be an endangered species in this world of agile?*

Today, most agile organizations are doing things in a more responsible manner— and they're doing them without managers. Now the questions arising- Where do Mangers fit in, in this type of culture?

Managers using old methodology can limit both the productivity of the team and the power of agile. While managing in a way that builds self-organization can be a challenge. But before we declare managers extinct, getting rid of managers isn't the solution to boosting productivity. However, the traditional approach to the management role needs to change. What we're actually seeing is the rise of a more skilled form of management. A manager's prime focus shouldn't be to manage, it should be to help and facilitate, to motivate and coach the team. In other words, what growing organizations need are leaders, not managers.

Redefine your Role

- Empowering over command
- Transparency over privacy
- Network over Hierarchies
- Experimental over Planning

Empowering over command

Traditional management often relies more on command rather than influence. For agile teams, the opposite needs to be true. Using influence can often be more effective in the long term in any organization, but it's essential on an agile team. A command culture can hinder a team's ability to develop self-organizational skills, which are at the heart of the value agile brings to an organization.

Traditional: Assigning individual's to-do list.

Agile: Empowering the team with skills.

Transparency over privacy

The traditional approach, the project manager is holding the helm of the project, thus others don't get to make the decisions. In agile methodology, everything is out there and transparent. The clients and decision makers are actively involved from the initiation, planning, review, and in the testing part of a product.

Traditional: Others have no say in decision making.

Agile: Transparency plays a significant role to constitute a healthy Agile environment.

Network over Hierarchies

In networked organizations, people work in a self-managed way. The managers have become enablers of self-managing teams and networks rather than controllers of individuals

Traditional: Organizing work through the authority

Agile: Organizing work through mutual understanding

Experimental over Planning

An agile mindset understands failure is natural and build a home for improvement, and early failure is like a cherry on the cake as it teaches us what does and doesn't work as soon as possible. It also recognizes there is no clear path to success and innovation, and the team has to find its way through constant experimentation and adapting to a new way of looking at the problem. In Traditional management, failing is not seen as an option, hence there is no easy way to deal with it when we encounter the same.

Traditional: Fixed scope.

Agile: Empirical mind-set, Flexible scope,

What do Agile Managers do?

1. The Manager becomes a facilitator and change agent / servant leader / chaos controller
2. Coaching Agile teams –Creating Agile Teams is one thing and having them follow agile effective is another matter entirely. In other words, leading and coaching the team becomes significantly important.
3. Managing budgets
4. Recruiting
5. Setting expectations– Benchmarking and monitoring expectations, doing periodic reviews.
6. Putting out fires – As the manager, it's still your responsibility to resolve all the conflicts and put the team on smooth track without hampering the productivity.
7. Manager can work as Agile Coach, scrum Master, Product Owner or as DEV Team member based on business needs.

So in all, I don't see Mangers getting extinct, we just need to put the cap of Agility to redefine the role of Manager. Agile Manager can help the team thrive, but without proper guidance about what it means to be a manager in an agile organization, management can have an adverse effect.

1.1.114. Agile Estimation and Planning at Program and Portfolio Level

Is there any relation between Estimation and Commitment? Absolutely not; Estimation is an approximate calculation, an educated guess, a prediction of a quantity, amount, extent or a value of something. Whereas, commitment is the willingness to give your time and energy to something that you believe in, or a promise or firm decision to do something. Now, Is there a relation between Estimation and Forecasting? Definitely yes; forecasting is to predict or estimate (a future event or trend).

In project teams; quite often estimation is considered as commitment, for which teams start spending too much time to get lot of details to get their estimates accurately. For one such reason, in 2011

Scrum Guide has removed the term "commit" in favor of "forecast" in regard to the work selected for a Sprint.

Estimations are based on experience and information available at our disposal at that time with a known fact that all factors pertaining to our prediction or projection are either unclear or unknown. However, when other factors such as cost, time, business value, and time to market step in, estimates should become more accurate and contribute to the business success. In other words, estimation at every instance of a project, from the task level till the release, decides the fate of a project and the business at large.

Estimations are more difficult to deal with in Agile projects where requirements evolve dynamically, schedules are nailed-down, scope is volatile, stakes are high, and teams are distributed. Also, estimates set expectations and if the outcome varies either with time or with respect to features, it will result in losses which will have a magnified effect. Hence in the agile world, besides being empirical, estimations should also be evolving and adaptive.

Advocates of classical estimation methods such as Function Point Analysis (FPA) might take this empirical approach with a pinch (or a bunch!) of salt. While classical estimation methods need well defined requirements and try to reduce the possibility of uncertainty, Agile methodologies nurture change requests as important challenge, readily accept uncertainty and try to address it moving in a diametrically opposite direction. Traditional estimating approach follows a "big-bang" task-based approach where the managers/leads develop a work breakdown structure with a list of tasks representing all the features and then estimate the hours each task would possibly consume. Once done, these estimates are considered final and don't necessarily change throughout the project. However, the actual effort will change, and the rest of the project is spent adjusting and bridging the gap between the estimated and actual hours.

Agile estimations, on the other hand, are feature-based with a focus on relative size of the prioritized features where the team comes up with an initial estimate and get started with the objective of presenting a working product or prototype to the client immediately. And as the project progresses and more clarity emerge on the features, the estimations are adjusted accordingly. And as time progresses, each iteration should imbibe and incorporate the lessons learnt from previous iterations and releases, creating self-correcting, self-regulating estimates that are based in reality. Such reality-based estimations enable the clients to continuously monitor the course of the projects, providing timely feedback thereby equipping the teams to constantly correct their plans and estimates.

Agile Estimating and Planning at Portfolio level

Illustrates the Agile Portfolio Planning Process.

Agile portfolio planning (or portfolio management) is an activity for determining which products or projects to work on, in which order, and for how long. The reality is that agile portfolio planning is a never-ending activity. As long as a company has products to develop or maintain, that company has a portfolio to manage. Portfolio planning has two outputs: a portfolio backlog and a set of active products. A portfolio backlog is similar to a product backlog; however, while a product backlog contains items relevant to only one product, a portfolio backlog describes multiple products, programs, or projects for which development has been approved but not yet begun. Each portfolio backlog item in the portfolio backlog might be a product, a product increment (one release of a product), or a project.

When estimating the size of portfolio backlog items, organizations should look for accuracy, not precision, because they will have a very limited amount of data when these initial estimates are made. An effective and quick way to accurately predict product size is to use the T-Shirt Size estimates. T-shirt sizing is based on the concept of binning. The bins are typically assigned labels corresponding to those commonly used with T-shirt sizes: extra small, small, medium, large, extra-large, etc. Frequently a cost range is associated with each size (e.g., an extra small project will cost between $10k and $25k) to provide organization-specific meaning to each T-shirt size. These measurements are accurate enough for decision making but not so precise as to be wasteful and most likely wrong.

Agile Estimating and Planning at Program/Product level

In Agile environments, plans evolve progressively. So, should estimates. We've features or requirements that need to be estimated starting from project, release and at sprint levels. Agile methodologies employ a simple and effective technique of expressing a requirement as a "user story".

Each user story above has different level of significance either in terms of time, cost, value and convenience.

User stories will be listed down in the Product Backlog and the team starts picking up user stories in the order of priority, starting from highest and start planning and estimating them.

Estimations occur and change throughout the projects, depending on the situation at hand. Teams need to do some initial estimating because at the beginning of iteration, they need to indicate what they think they're going to deliver (user stories picked up for that iteration), how they're going to do so (task breakdown from user stories), and how long they think it will take (about an epic spanning across iterations). Because of the inherent uncertainty in the information at the beginning of a project, we'll need to give "ranged" answers at first and then tighten up the answers as the project progresses.

In Agile, we follow a simple rule: The people who will do the work (the development team) collectively provide the estimates. Because everyone on the development team sees the story from a different perspective, it's essential that all members of the development team participate during estimation.

Relative Size Estimation

Estimate User Stories/PBI's using relative sizes, not absolute sizes. In other words, determine how large each item is relative to others. People are much more accurate at gauging relative measures (e.g., halfway there or a one-third) than they are at absolute measures (e.g., 10 feet or 6 kgs).

Story Points

Story points are a unit of measure for expressing an estimate of the overall effort that will be required to fully implement a product backlog item or any other piece of work. When we estimate with story points, we assign a point value to each item. The raw values we assign are unimportant. What matters are the relative values. A story that is assigned a 2 should be twice as much as a story that is assigned a 1. It should also be two-thirds of a story that is estimated as 3 story points. Planning Poker is helpful to size the PBIs in Story Points.

Because story points represent the effort to develop a story, a team's estimate must include everything that can affect the effort. That could include:

- ➢ The amount of work to do
- ➢ The complexity of the work
- ➢ Any risk or uncertainty in doing the work
- ➢ Definition of Done

Ideal Days

An alternative approach for measuring PBIs is to use ideal days—the number of effort-days or person-days needed to complete a story. Ideal time is not the same as elapsed time. A football game would be measured as 60 minutes in ideal time (4, 15-minute quarters), but the elapsed time is closer to 3.5 to 4 hours. The main drawback of ideal time is that it can be misinterpreted as elapsed time, which creates confusion and frustration.

Conclusion: Often, teams transitioning to agile find it hard switching from the traditional task-based predictive estimates to feature-based speculative estimates and question the benefit in making a painful transition. As estimations set expectations, initially the teams might experience hiccups, but as the sprints or iterations progress, estimations become more pragmatic and hence more accurate. Thus, Estimations can help teams make significant decisions, get better understanding of stories, gain an insight on design and architectural directions in future. There's no fixed time or short cuts defined for the teams to get better at estimations. Each team's approach to estimation evolves as the project progresses; first they struggle with estimation, then can get quite good at it, and then probably reach a point where they often don't need it as higher trust levels lead to lesser estimation effort.

1.1.115. Is there a PMO in your organization?
- ○ Yes - a single office
- ○ Yes - more than one office
- ○ Yes - there is someone with a PMO title
- ○ No
- ○ I don't know
- ○ Other (please specify)

1.1.116. Was there a PMO before the transition to Agile?
- ○ Yes, with the same role and responsibilities.
- ○ Yes, but the roles and responsibilities have changed.
- ○ No.
- ○ I don't know.
- ○ Other (please specify)

1.1.117. Which Methodology, Framework or group of methodologies are used in your organization? (You can select more than one)
- ○ Adaptive Software Development (ASD)
- ○ Agile Modelling
- ○ Feature-driven Development (FDD)
- ○ Dynamic systems development method (DSDM)
- ○ Internet-speed development (ISD)
- ○ Scrum
- ○ Lean
- ○ Extreme Programming (XP)
- ○ Crystal
- ○ Scaled Agile Framework (SAFe)
- ○ Large Scale Scrum (LeSS)

- o Disciplined Agile Delivery (DA 2.0 or DAD)
- o Tribes/Spotify
- o Scrum of Scrums (SoS)
- o Nexus
- o Other (please specify)

1.1.118. Who should write the user story? Product Owner? Development Team? Anyone? What is your answer?

1.1.119. What is the business value addition of "Face-to-Face Collaboration" in agile team?

1.1.120. What is the business value addition of "Face-to-Face Collaboration" in agile team?

It increases team's cohesiveness, increases team's velocity, collaboration and efficiency and enhances customers delight by delivering shippable products increments iteratively.

1.1.121. Explain five common anti-patterns of inflicting help by Scrum Master?

Scrum Masters should STOP inflicting help on teams. Here are five common anti-patterns of inflicting help

1. Scrum Master as a "meeting master" - Sends the meeting invites, booking the meeting room, opening the conference bridge - Why can the team not take ownership of these (maybe, with just the exception of Sprint Review where it would be more appropriate for the PO to invite the right stakeholders)?

2. Excessive focus (obsession?) only at the team level (sometimes team + Product Owner) and not focusing on the organization)

3. The baby-sitter - makes themselves indispensable to the team by directly or indirectly creating dependencies on the SM (example - team does not start the Daily Scrum till the SM shows up, or asks the team to start)

4. The over-zealous impediment remover - Does not even let the team come in terms with the impediment, let alone have them self-organize to tackle it first. Jumps right away on it after hearing the word "impediment"

5. The Team Admin - Take meeting notes for the team? Done. Write a User Story? Done. Update JIRA? Done. Update Burndown chart? Done

1.1.121. Explain Scrum Master tips on dot voting technique?

Are you using dot voting? There is a major flaw in how dot voting *usually* gets facilitated. All votes need to be unbiased. But in reality, people placing the dots towards the end can get biased by dots already placed (and they can change their mind to the last minute by looking at the patterns). This approach is flawed. Have you seen this before? Or experienced it yourself as a participant?

It can be rectified by first having people WRITE DOWN their individual choices concurrently and privately, say, on a post-it notes (so it is unbiased), then place the votes by showing their written choices. (Or, the facilitator can call out individually asking for the participants' choices, they still show their post-it's to the group). This way, dot voting will be more unbiased. This can be used for weighted dot voting as well (votes have unequal weights, and different colours correspond to different weights).

1.1.122. Explain 5 useful tips for successful Agile transformation?

1. Establish a guiding coalition that will start the transformation studies and lead it up to a certain point. This coalition should determine the transformation vision, lead the strategic steps towards this vision, provide guidance to the organization for the implementation of transformation efforts, and increase the visibility of all these studies.
Agility is a culture transformation that is far more than just a set of practices to be applied at the team level. It means that the company's entire way of working evolves into a whole new form. An important part of this is the process of managers' transformation into next-generation servant leaders, leaving their old chain of command understanding and practices.

2. Focus on training and coaching studies at the management level for your managers to abandon their old and traditional management habits and become the next generation Agile leaders. Start transformation studies not only by focusing on your teams, but also the management.

3. In order to accelerate and advance in the medium term, one must start slowly. Start a transformation in a strategically important but relatively small part of the organization. Following your experiences here, extend the transformation studies to the entire organization.

4. Create internal competency-based and/or practice-oriented communities. Invest in these communities to make them functional and sustainable. Authorize these communities to be part of the transformation. Thus, you can have an organization where people not only share something but also take actions.

5. Begin by setting up a small Agile Coach community consisting of experienced and eager people in your organization like Agile team members, Scrum Master, and Product Owner. Train and guide this community with the support of outside experts. At least some of them will be your successful agents of internal transformation in the future.

1.1.123. Explain some useful tips for successful daily stand-up meetings?

a. Identify the mistakes

It's not a status call. There should be one common shared vision on daily stand-up meetings among scrum teams.

b. Keep meetings short and simple with specified agenda.

c. Get your meetings off to the best possible start with prior relevant home works of team members on an index card about their work.

d. Don't be afraid to acknowledge constraints, use prompts to encourage them to speak up.

e. Make sure that attendance levels are high.

f. Make sure everyone is heard.

g. Don't be afraid to change things as relevant.

1.1.124. How to work with difficult people?

"When dealing with people, remember you are not dealing with creatures of logic, but with creatures of emotion, creatures bristling with prejudice, and motivated by pride and vanity"

- Dale Carnegie

1.1.125. What are the different coaching models currently available in market?

Some of the currently available coaching models are mentioned below. But we need to know the context and which model we need to use when.

- o GROW
- o TGROW
- o OSKAR
- o OUTCOMES
- o SPACE
- o ACHIEVE
- o POSITIVE.

1.1.126. What are the coaching KATA questions for improvement?

Here, are the five coaching KATA questions for improvement.

a. What is the target condition?
b. What is the actual condition now?
c. What obstacles are now preventing you from achieving the desired final condition?
d. What is your next step (PDCA experiment)?
e. Step back, learn, improve, sustain and reuse. When users can go and inspect your lessons learnt at a particular step?

1.1.127. What are the seven habits of highly empathetic coach?

Here, are the seven habits of highly empathetic coach.

a. Getting curious about strangers
b. Active listening and being vulnerable
c. Offer your support
d. Practice emotional detachment
e. Be fully present when you are with people
f. Try following another person's life
g. Ask better effective questions.

1.1.128. What are the tips to coach for greatness?

"I absolutely believe that people, unless coached, never reach their maximum capabilities".

- Bob Nardelli

1.1.129. What are the common characteristics of a self-organized team?

A self-organized team should have the below characteristics.

a. They are autonomous
b. They have a common purpose
c. They learn from each other continuously
d. They take ownership of their job/activity/task
e. They share and care for each other's
f. They are leader - leader on their own (shared leadership).

1.1.130. What are the points to look at while building Agile culture?

While building Agile culture We need to look at eight points.

a. Look for the opportunities where you can appreciate others

b. Help individuals where he/she can perform better and you can appreciate
c. Share the common goal with the team members and share the expectations. Help them to set stretch goals.
d. Create an appreciation platform. Make it shorter and frequent.
e. Create 4C's mechanism within stakeholders. Connect, collaborate, communicate and celebrate.
Create many ways for appreciation, e.g., writing best code, share best stories, helping others in crisis situation, best support team members, creative team members, blue thanks, kudos, pat on back etc.
f. Celebrate the achievements.
g. Make it visual, on the board where all the team members can see. Make it user-friendly and self-explanatory.
h. Recognize best ideas, best solutions, best knowledge shared etc.

Recognize the skills, knowledge, behaviours and demeanour that supports Lean agile performance to reinforce them at all levels of the organization.
A culture of recognition engages, energizes and empowers employees.

1.1.131. What are the techniques to look at while building intuition?

Mitchell and Stevens recommend these four techniques to help you building intuition.

a. Meditate
b. Do a blind reading
c. Play red-light green-light
d. Learn more through readings and classes.

1.1.132. How can we sustain any change initiative?

Some pointers are articulated below.

a. Have a focus group with experts, who can bring and effectively implement those changes smoothly
b. Let us have a periodic review on the changes and improvements / outcomes achieved in the organization and communicate with all the stakeholders
c. Connect with stakeholders, understand their concerns/ pain areas, collaborate
d. Series of communication at different levels and get the feedback
e. Engage different ways to engage stakeholders to participate. Facilitate those events to connect with the people.
f. Let us talk openly, stakeholders voice and concern in a common area so that there is no secret mission.
g. Build win-win situation wherever possible
h. Take the help from all the team members wherever possible. Slowly resistance will become cooperation.

We need to keep looking and calibrate the situation for sustaining the changes for long.

1.1.133. What skills the Project Manager needs to unlearn in the Agile world?

The below skills Project Manager needs to unlearn in the Agile world.

a. Command and control mindset
b. Plan driven mindset, Upfront planning attitude for all things
c. Less experimental mindset
d. Less adaptability
e. Too much process focussed mindset
f. Outdated Project and Product development knowledge
g. Uncomfortable with ambiguity.

1.1.134. What are the major challenges generally faced while creating Agile Centre of excellence (CoE)?

Some of the challenges could be

a. Less budget for CoE build and set up
b. Insufficient competency
c. Internal power conflicts
d. Complaints from other business units
e. Not able to provide customized "FIT-FOR-PURPOSE" solution at the right time as per business needs.

1.1.135. Name different activities learning organizations are skilled in?

Learning organizations are skilled in five main activities.

a. Systematic problem solving
b. Experimentation with new approaches
c. Learning from their past experiences and lessons learnt
d. Learning from the experiences and best practices of others
e. Transferring the assets, lessons learnt and best practices docs to the organization for reusability purposes.

1.1.136. Name key enablers to improve coaching?

Some of the key enablers to improve coaching are articulated below (irrespective of any coaching model).

a. Communicate shared common vision and clear expectations in team
b. Build relationships
c. Give feedback on areas that require specific improvement(s)
d. Help to remove impediments
e. Listen actively

f. Groom, give gentle advice and guidance
g. Give emotional support including empathy
h. Reflect content or meaning
i. Effective questioning techniques
j. Gain a commitment to change
k. Applaud good results.

1.1.137. Mention the different surprising techniques used by agile team to write better user stories in less time with less aggravation?

1. Technique 1 - Have quarterly story-writing workshop having significant objective. Focus on one goal on MVP (minimum viable product) and on MMF (minimum marketable product).

2. Technique 2 - Master the art of splitting stories.

3. Technique 3 - Add just enough detail, just in time.

1.1.138. Mention the 3 qualities of potentially releasable or shippable product increment?

Top 3 qualities of potentially releasable or shippable product increment are -

a. High quality
b. Properly tested
c. What it does, it does well.

1.1.139. What is development team?

Development Team is a Cross-Functional (all product development skills like development, testing, analysis, design etc. in the same team) and self-organizing (empowered to make decisions about how to build the product). The team is responsible for delivering a quality product with the guidance of the Product Owner.

1.1.140. Quiz Session

Questions

1. Which practice does not fall under Technical best practices?

Select the correct answer.
A. Automated build & Continuous Integration
B. Automated Regression Testing
C. Code Review & Rework
D. None of the above

2. Retrospective meetings help us to_____.

Select the correct answer.
A. Identify areas of improvement
B. Recognize team members
C. Inspect and adapt
D. All of the above

3. Sprint backlog is updated by _____.

Select the correct answer.
A. Scrum Master
B. Scrum Team
C. Scrum Product Owner
D. Any of the above

4. Product Owner has to mandatorily participate in Daily Scrum Meeting.

Select the correct answer.
A. Yes
B. No
C. Not required
D. Based on needs

5. Which life cycle model does the Agile method follow:

Select the correct answer.
A. Waterfall model
B. Iterative and Incremental model
C. V-model
D. None of the above

6. Product backlog contains prioritized_____ .

Select the correct answer.
A. Epics
B. User stories
C. Epics and user stories
D. None of the above

7. Which of the following roles is not defined by Scrum?

Select the correct answer.
A. Product Owner
B. Project Manager
C. Developer / Tester
D. Scrum Master

Answers

1.	D
2.	D
3.	B
4.	D
5.	B
6.	C
7.	B

NOTES

NOTES

NOTES

NOTES

Chapter 2 - Introduction

DevOps is an approach based on the Lean and Agile principles in which business owners and the development, operations, and quality assurance departments collaborate to deliver IT solutions in a continuous manner that enables the business to seize market opportunities more quickly and reduce the time to include customer feedback.

- DevOps is a collaborative way of developing and deploying software.
- DevOps is a set of practices that provides rapid and reliable software delivery.
- DevOps is a movement that improves IT service delivery agility.
- DevOps is a set of practices that provides rapid, reliable software delivery.
- DevOps is a culture that promotes better working relationship within the company.
- DevOps is an environment that promotes cross practicality, shared business tasks and belief.

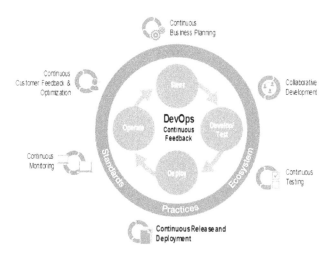

Figure 2.1 : DevOps in a nutshell

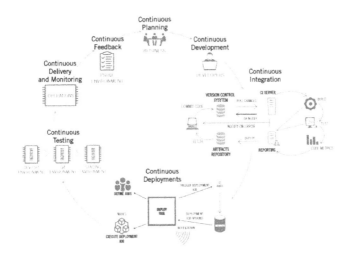

Figure 2.2 : DevOps in IT

Patrick Debois introduced DevOps in 2009; he is often known as *the father of DevOps*.

Need of DevOps: Developers want to deliver changes as soon as possible, but operations want reliability and stability.

Lee Thomson named it as a wall of confusion between the software developers and IT operations.

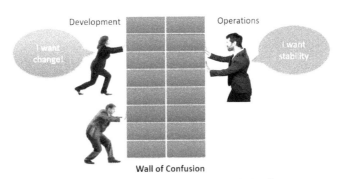

Figure 2.3 : Wall of Confusion silos

- The wall of confusion exists between the mind-set of both the teams and also within the tools they use.

- DevOps helps to break this wall of confusion, unifying the development to operations for better and for faster outcomes.

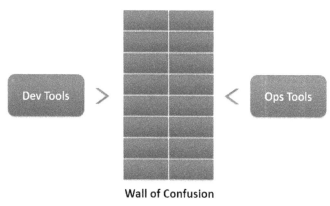

Wall of Confusion

Figure 2.4 : Wall of Confusion

But DevOps is not:

a. Just limited to cloud
b. A role
c. Just confined to development
d. Just agile
e. Just for developers
f. Automation only

2.1. DevOps Interview questions and answers

2.1.1. Principles of DevOps

- Business value for end user
- People Integration Metrics, KPI
- Ideas, Plans, Goals, Metrics, Complications, Tools
- Performance Metrics, Logs, Business goals Metrics,
- Continuous Delivery, Continuous Monitoring, Configuration Management
- Eliminate blame game, Open post-mortems, Feedback, Rewarding failures

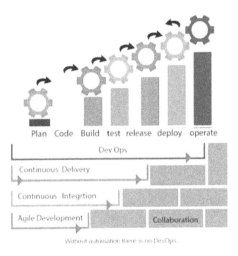

Figure 2.5 : DevOps Principles

2.1.2. Key Components of DevOps

- **Controlled Process (CP)**
- **Continuous Integration (CI)**
- **Continuous Deployment (CD)**
- **Continuous Testing (CT)**
- **Continuous Monitoring (CM)**
- Communication & Collaboration
- People – Communication & Collaboration
- Process – Source Control Check-ins, Code Review & Quality, Change Control, RCAs

Figure 2.6 : DevOps – Key Components

2.1.3. DevOps Capabilities

- Automate Provisioning – Infrastructure as Code
- Automate Builds – Continuous Integration
- Automate Deployments – Defined Deployment Pipeline and
- Continuous Deployments with appropriate configurations for the environments
- Automate Testing – Continuous Testing, Automated tests after each deployment
- Automate Monitoring – Proper monitors in place sending alerts
- Automate Metrics – Performance Metrics, Logs

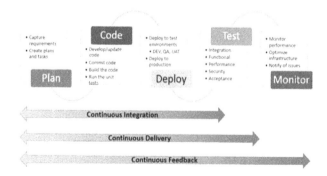

Figure 2.7 : DevOps Capabilities

- **Six DevOps Capabilities**

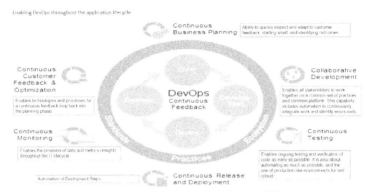

Figure 2.8 : DevOps – Six Capabilities

2.1.4. DevOps Purpose & Objectives

DevOps combines the best of all teams providing
- Minimizes rollbacks
- Reduces Deployment related downtime
- Increases Virtualize Environments utilization
- Develops and verifies against production-like systems
- Increases Quality – Automated testing, Reduce cost/time to test
- Reduces Defect cycle time – Increase the ability to reproduce and fix defects
- Reduces cost/time to deliver – Deploy often & faster with repeatable, reliable process

2.1.5. DevOps Triggering Points

- Need to reduce IT costs
- Need to improve the end customer experience
- The increasing need to develop or deploy cloud based applications
- A greater need for simultaneous deployment across different platforms
- The need for greater collaboration between development and operations terms
- An increasingly complex IT infrastructure that is part physical, part virtualized, and part cloud
- Pressures from business to release applications more quickly to meet customer demand or enter new markets

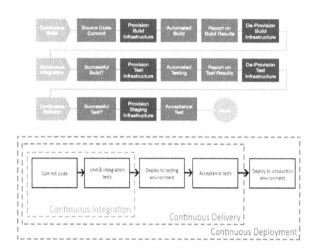

Figure 2.9 : What drives the needs of DevOps

2.1.6. DevOps and People, Process and Technology

- DevOps is a culture which promotes collaboration between Development and Operations Team to deploy code to production faster in an automated and repeatable way. The word 'DevOps' is a combination of two words *development* and *operations.*
- A way of working – a combination of: *People, Process & Tools*
- DevOps is a *philosophy* of the *efficient development, deployment and operation,* of the highest quality software possible.
- An alignment of development and IT operations with better communication and collaboration.
- About *eliminating inefficiencies & bottlenecks* in the software delivery lifecycle.
- DevOps is an *approach based on Lean and Agile principles* in which business owners and the development, operations, quality assurance departments collaborate to deliver software in a continuous manner that enables the business to more quickly seize market opportunities and *reduce the time to include customer feedback.*

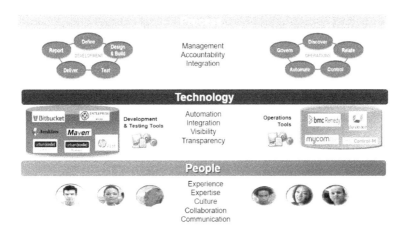

Figure 2.10 : DevOps – People, Process and Technology

DevOps is a culture that promotes the following:

- People first, then Process and then Technology (PPT)
- Better working relationship within the company
- Continual experimentation, which requires taking risks and learning from success and failure
- Understanding that the repetition and practice are the prerequisites to mastery

2.1.7. DevOps "Why" & "What"

a. What's in it for Individuals

- Get involved in the end to end process of developing, testing & delivering the business features to clients.
- Monitoring how these features are performing.
- Accept more responsibility in turn getting credit for the value they bring to clients.
- Have better understanding of the role, their work & code play for the product & business.
- Rich technical learning experience.
- Learn industry transforming technologies, product and enhance their technical abilities, making them competitive.

b. **Why should Customer adopt DevOps**

- DevOps was the Mantra for success yesterday/ it is the mantra for survival today.
- You would be obsolete even if you think you would look at it in six months.
- The business cannot compete in the market if it cannot deliver faster in a continuous way on day to day basis.
- Customer is expecting immediate resolution of his/her feedback – immediate is NOW.
- Every Business is linked in some way with CAMS and the end customer expectations are 'everything now'.

2.1.8. DevOps – Key Takeaways

The needs for DevOps must be driven for Business.

- We covered this still anyway here we go.
- DevOps is not Automation but Automation is the stepping stone in the DevOps adoption.
- DevOps is a combination of culture, processes, and tools.
- Automation, if not continuous will not help.
- Automation at every stage when integrated to the next stage resulting into continuous delivery, that is DevOps!

DevOps is not:

- Just limited to cloud
- A role
- Just confined to development
- Just agile
- Just for developers
- Automation only

DevOps is much more than agile:

- DevOps is complementary to agile
- Agile focuses on the software development process
- DevOps extends and completes the continuous integration and release process

DevOps – Technical Benefits
- Continuous software delivery
- Less complexity
- Faster issue resolutions

DevOps – Business Benefits
- Faster delivery of features
- More stable operating environment
- Improved communication & collaboration
- More time to innovate

DevOps – Cultural Benefits
- Happier, more productive teams
- Higher employee engagement
- Greater professional development opportunities
- Integrated process and teams

2.1.9. DevOps – Impediments

It doesn't matter whether you are in Cloud, Enterprise or Mobile.
For each of *Stable Software Delivery*, *On-Time* is the key to business success.

Key Challenges for Implementing DevOps Strategy
- **Production downtime**: to lack of improper deployment instructions / checklist.
- **No proper SCM management**: Discrepancies in managing configurations, No Code Baseline management.
- Broken Build, Deployment, Continuous Integration, Continuous Testing framework ➔ SaaS Managed Apps.
- **Hacking**: Fixing directly in PROD (instead of a proper hotfix process) and forgets to check-in into source control.
- No Environment Strategy and Principles. Each Vendor/Provider has its own concept/rule to manage Environment / process.
- **Deployments are a blocker**: Upgrade risk due to manual management of multiple application configuration and versions, Dependency on specific deployment SME.

Key Issues Blocking Software Delivery?
- No shared ownership – Lack of feedback and proper metric leads
- Slow deployments – Costly error prone manual process and efforts
- Building and maintaining servers – Time consuming and unproductive
- No environment management - Differences in development and production environments

Key obstacles in implementing DevOps in an organization?
- Tools don't work well together.
- It's unknown, not testified, must be too expensive!!

- I can't get my management to buy into new processes.
- The value of DevOps isn't understood outside my group.
- DevOps is too new and I don't have the support, I need to be successful.
- There is no common management structure between development and operations.
- Its someone's action or dream or an organization initiative, I would go as per traditional norms.

2.1.10.   DevOps – Value Stream Example

Illustrated with an example view of **Value realization**, once DevOps solution is implemented covering all aspects *People, Process, Application, Tools, Methods* and so on.

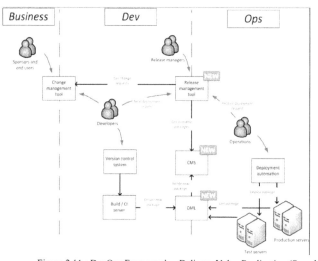

Figure 2.11 : DevOps Framework – Delivery Value Realization (Sample)

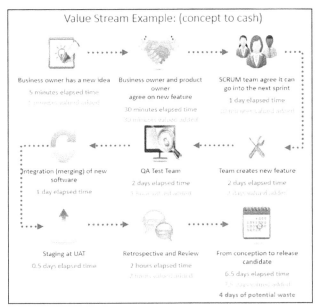

Figure 2.12 : DevOps – Value stream example – Concept to cash

2.1.11.   DevOps Framework – Definitions and Overview

Why DevOps

Business Benefits

- Faster delivery of features
- More stable operating environment
- Improved communication & collaboration
- More time to innovate

Technical Benefits
- Continuous software delivery
- Less complexity
- Faster issue resolutions

Cultural Benefits
- Happier, more productive teams
- Higher employee engagement
- Greater professional development opportunities
- Integrated process and teams

- Before DevOps, the development and operation team worked in complete isolation.
- Testing and Deployment were isolated activities done after design-build. Hence, they consumed more time than actual build cycles.
- Without using DevOps, team members are spending a *large amount of their time in testing, and deploying* instead of building the project.
- Manual code deployment leads to *human errors* in production.
- Coding & operation teams have their separate timelines and are not in *sync* causing further delays.
- There is a demand to increase *the rate of software delivery* by business stakeholders.

As per Forrester Consulting Study, Only 17% of teams can use delivery software fast enough. This proves the PAIN POINT.

2.1.12.   DevOps follows CALMS model

C ulture	• Hearts and minds • Embrace change
A utomation	• CI / CD • Infrastructure as code
L ean	• Focus on production value for the end-user • Small batch sizes
M easurement	• Measure everything • Show the improvement
S haring	• Open information sharing • Collaboration

2.1.13.   DevOps – Work Practices vs Phase

- DevOps takes and end-to-end approach of software delivery.
- Previous practices (<u>example</u>: Agile) addressed only a subset of value chain.

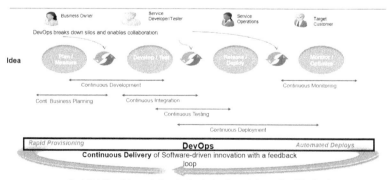

Figure 2.13 : DevOps "Capability Framework Model"

2.1.14. DevOps – Work Products

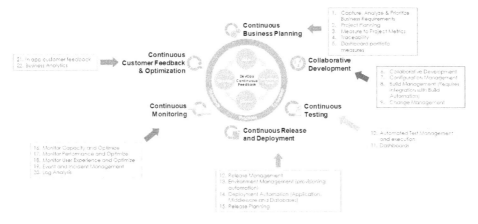

Figure 2.14 : 6C's and 22 Principles of DevOps

2.1.15. DevOps Practice - Continuous Business Planning

A. **Key opportunities or pain which can be addressed by this practice**
- Requirement Traceability from source to production deployment.
- Phase wise release planning in multiple sprints.
- Adoption to Lean design thinking
- Plan to adopt the Delivery Pipeline in the Blue mix Continuous Delivery.
- Teams needs to be guided on culture, best DevOps practices, tools, self-guided or hands-on training—even sample code and architectures for developers.
- Transform the team from slow, siloed teams to a self-managing, solution-oriented, bottleneck-free, go-fast team.
- Operations should measure not only the enhancement in speed of releases but also the impact of the changes deployments on budget and on customer value.

B. **Primary set of tools which can be used to effectively implement this Practice**
- JIRA
- RTVM
- Muller, CA Agile
- Tool Chain
- IBM Rational Team Concert

C. **Key Business & IT benefits which can be driven from this practice**
- Acceptance Criteria can be defined as business outcome rather than just IT test cases execution
- Change traceability from requirements to production

- Ensuring Robust integrated solutions to the overall delivery at each phase of application development and its operations.
- Using Agile methodology, DEV team(s) are able to shorten development cycles dramatically and increase application quality.

2.1.16.   DevOps Practice - Collaborative Development

A. **Key Opportunities or Pain which can be addressed by this practice**
- The overall integration effort is reduced by integrating the system more frequently and it is easier to fix recurring issues.
- Change sets from all developers are integrated in a team workspace, and then built and unit tested frequently. This should happen at least daily, but ideally it happens any time a new change set is available.
- Integrate and automate build, deploy, testing, and promotion to obtain quick resolutions to the issues identified.
- Team to be collaborated via communication tools for each set of changes on build.
- Developers must develop the discipline and skills to organize their work into small, cohesive change sets.

B. **Primary set of Tools which can be used to effectively implement this Practice**

- RTVM
- GIT HUB
- HP –UFT
- ALM
- IBM Box
- HipChat
- Confluence
- BitBucket
- IBM Connections
- IBM Verse
- Slack
- Jenkins
- IBM Urban Code Build
- IBM Rational Collaborative Lifecycle Management (CLM)

C. **Key Business & IT benefits which can be driven from this Practice**
- The result is a higher quality product and more predictable delivery schedules.
- Changes are made to a configuration that is known to be good and tested before the new code is available.
- Improved error detection.
- Integrate and test the system on every change to minimize the time between injecting a defect and correcting it.
- By integrating continuously throughout the project, continuous build happens for each set of changes, thereby mitigating integration surprises at the end of the lifecycle.

2.1.17. DevOps Practice - Continuous Testing

A. **Key Opportunities or Pain which can be addressed by this practice**
- Requirement traceability for each test cases.
- Regression suite pack automation and auto execution after each build being system tested.
- Cognitive approach to do predictive analysis on defects.
- Defect management - Daily checkpoints on defects fixes with all integration interfaces stakeholders.
- Cognitive analytics to produce the periodical frequent dashboard

B. **Primary set of Tools which can be used to effectively implement this Practice**
- RTVM
- Muller, CA Agile
- Selenium
- ALM, Win runner ,
- Tool chain
- JUnit
- Cognitive – Watson explorer
- Rational Test Virtualization Server
- IBM Worklight Quality Assurance

C. **Key Business & IT benefits which can be driven from this practice**
- Acceptance Criteria can be defined as business outcome after each build being executed for testing.
- Staged builds will provide a useful means to organize testing to get the right balance between coverage and speed.
- Predictive analysis dashboard with current health of project and future prediction can alarm client at every stage on the state of the product delivery.
- Using DevOps insights, one can explore project's defects data by viewing the dashboards in the data category.

2.1.18. DevOps Practice - Continuous Deployments

A. **Key Opportunities or Pain which can be addressed by this practice**
- Team can be more productive, less stressed, and more focused on feature delivery rather than dealing with big, unknown potential changes.
- If every change is releasable, it has to be entirely self-contained. That includes things like user documentation, operations runbooks, and information about exactly what changed and how for audits and traceability.
- Deliver through an automated pipeline.

- Automate not only builds and code deployments, but even the process of constructing new development, test, and production environments.
- Implement blue-green deployments.
- Pain area:
    - Difficult to automate the process of constructing new developments as the most of the applications hosted on premise environment using different technologies difficult to bring all together in automated way . Way forward would be to use Blue mix and find the scope of building API and connect the process with automation scripts.

B. **Primary set of tools which can be used to effectively implement this practice**
- RTVM
- Muller, CA Agile
- GIT HUB
- Tool chain
- ANT
- Bamboo
- Release management tools – SNOW, Remedy
- Docker
- IBM Urban code Deploy

C. **Key Business & IT benefits which can be driven from this Practice**
- Acceptance Criteria can be defined as business outcome after each build being executed for Testing.
- Staged builds will provide a useful means to organize testing to get the right balance between coverage and speed.
- The key to building a good delivery pipeline is to automate nearly everything in the development process.
- Aim for zero downtime.

2.1.19.   DevOps Practice - Continuous Monitoring

A. **Key Opportunities or Pain which can be addressed by this practice**
- Automated Monitoring tools to measure application response time every few minutes from around the globe.
- Most often, the dependencies that one application has on other components or services is not tracked regularly.
- Integrate automated monitoring with rich notification tooling.
- Access the efficiency of automated monitoring tools.
- Monitoring and analytics services on Bluemix.
- Pain area:
    - Automated monitoring leads to some form of failure or performance degradation due to the complexity of the applications.
- Solution: Use collaboration tools, such as Slack or Google Hangouts, to collectively solve problems with the help of SME's on various service areas involved.

B. **Primary set of tools which can be used to effectively implement this practice**
- ServiceNow, Remedy
- PagerDuty, Nettool (Netpin notification)
- Slack, Google hangout
- Control M, CRON jobs
- IBM Bluemix Availability monitoring
- IBM Monitoring and Analytics
- NewRelic, Pingdom,
- Datadog, Uptime, Sensu
- IBM Alert Notification
- Dynatrace
- AppDynamics
- Splunk, Sumologic

C. **Key Business & IT benefits which can be driven from this Practice**
- Quick identification of the root cause of an issue, through the use of line-of-code diagnostics.
- Faster time to resolve application's issue by using embedded analytics to search log and metric data.
- Good automated monitoring is being able to recognize trends that lead to a problem.
- Instant visibility and transparency into the application's performance and health without the need to learn or deploy other tools.
- Reduced maintenance costs, as the application keeps running with minimal effort.

2.1.20.   DevOps Practice - Continuous Customer Feedback and Optimization

A. **Key Opportunities or Pain which can be addressed by this practice**
- The most important metric to track in the cloud is time to recovery for any defect/ down time.
- In today's global marketplace, websites are expected to be always available.
- To meet the SLA goal, the Garage Method team took these actions:
  - o Implement a continuous delivery process by using IBM Blue mix Continuous Delivery.
  - o Implement a *Deploy to Test* stage.
  - o Implement blue-green deployment.
  - o Deploy the production website to multiple Blue mix data centers.
- Write and maintain runbooks to troubleshoot operational issues.
- Surface SLA reports that clearly show daily, weekly, and monthly outage data.

B. **Primary set of tools which can be used to effectively implement this practice**
- Runbook Automation
- Tool Chains
- Delivery Pipeline
- IBM Tea leaf
- IBM Smart Cloud Analytics—Log Analysis

C. **Key business & IT benefits which can be driven from this practice**
- Continuously gain new insights from the customers' interaction about the application and the metrics collected to drive business decisions.
- Shift operational practices to the front of the development cycle to improve reliability.
- DevOps is the leading way to develop and deliver competitive applications and solutions to the market.
- Deliver a differentiated and engaging customer experience that builds customer loyalty and increases market share by continuously obtaining and responding to customer feedback.
- Respond to the market faster and ensure an outstanding customer experience.
- Improving productivity through accelerated business feedback cycles

2.1.21.   DevOps "Capability Framework Model"

- DevOps takes an end-to-end approach of software delivery
- Previous practices (example: Agile) addressed only a subset of value chain

Goal: Get ideas into market/production fast, get people use it, get feedback

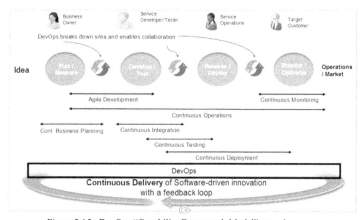

Figure 2.15 : DevOps "Capability Framework Model" overview

Figure 2.16 : DevOps "Capability Framework Model" illustration

2.1.22.　DevOps "Capability Framework Principles"

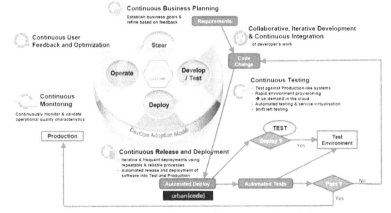

Figure 2.17 : DevOps "Capability Framework Principles"

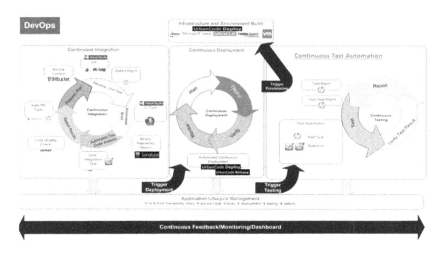

Figure 2.18 : DevOps "Capability Framework Principles" overview

2.1.23. DevOps "Operating Model" Framework

Please find it enclosed below.

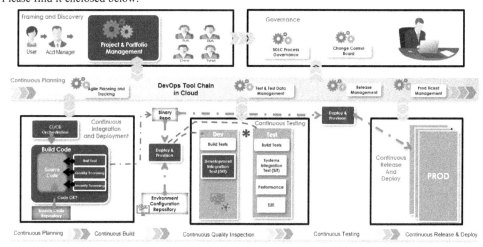

Figure 2.19: DevOps "Operating Model" Framework overview

Please tailor it as applicable based on your customer requirement.

2.1.24.   DevOps "Tools" with "SDLC Phases" - Demo

Picture illustrates with SDLC project delivery model, using *different tools* to integrate per Application/Product component to realize DevOps delivery solution model.

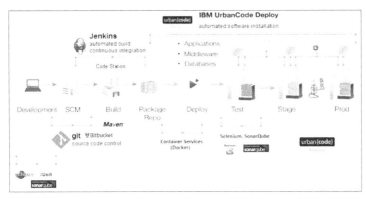

Figure 2.20 : DevOps "Tools" with "SDLC Phases" – Sample

2.1.25.   DevOps "Tooling Framework" – VALUE Chain DEMO

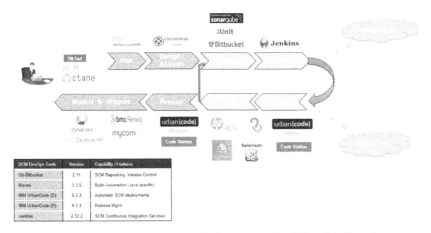

Figure 2.21 : DevOps "Tooling Framework" – Value Chain Example

2.1.26.   SDLC / ALM Framework- Phase & Tool Example - DEMO

The following picture illustrates with the SDLC/ALM phases, with its tools usage for DevOps framework (CI, CD) to manage expected outcomes.
Within SDLC/ALM, we also illustrate QA models using traditional, Agile and DevOps, on how "*QA benefits with built-in QC controls*" for DevOps.

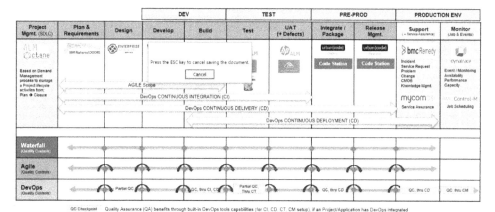

Figure 2.22: SDLC / ALM Framework – Phase & Tool Example

2.1.27. DevOps "Continuous Business Planning"

A simplified view across the development and delivery lifecycles
maximize business outcomes and value through an open collaborative, standards-based platform and strong governance framework.

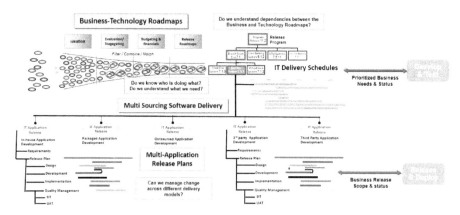

Figure 2.23: DevOps "Continuous Business Planning"

2.1.28.   DevOps "Continuous Integration & Continuous Testing"

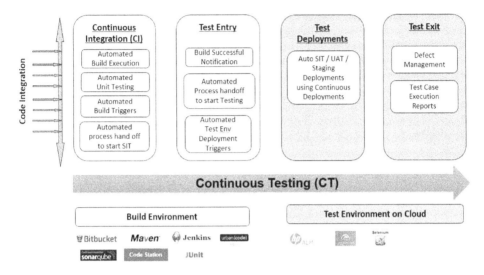

Figure 2.24: DevOps "Continuous Integration & Continuous Testing" overview

2.1.29.   DevOps "Continuous Deployment & Release Management"

It provides a continuous delivery pipeline which automate deployments to test on production like environments. It reduces the amount of manual labor, resource wait-time, and rework by means of push-button deployments that allow higher frequency of releases, reduced errors, and end-to-end transparency for compliance.

The continuous release and deployment practice within DevOps addresses existing problems in traditional software development, such as:

- Teams using different tools across the software development lifecycle
- Processes that do not scale to the complexity of applications
- Conflicts between development and operations

Continuous deployment is closely related to continuous integration and refers to the release into production of software that passes the automated tests.

Continuous Deploy

- Promoting multi-tiered SCM code through to production
- Versioning deployment artifacts
- Managing incremental deployment changes
- Deployments to middleware environments
- Database change deployments
- Deployment snapshots
- Rollbacks

Continuous release
- Manage environment changes in release events
- Track infrastructure and application changes through a release
- Orchestrate releases of inter-dependent applications
- Facilitate release collaborations

And it offers following benefits

- Speed time to market
- Stable and predictable releases
- Increased visibility
- Fewer outages & efficient rollbacks if required
- Release better software more often

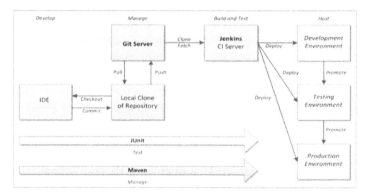

Figure 2.25: DevOps "Continuous Deployment & Release Management" overview

2.1.30.　　　DevOps "Continuous Release Management"

What's a Release?
Release is a workable software product labeled or named with some number or name.
It is produced to deliver specific requirements. It's normally incremental and produced out of SDLC phases.

2.1.31.　What's a Deployment?
The activity responsible for movement of approved releases of hardware, software, documentation, processes etc. to any environments.

2.1.32.　Release & Deployment Activities
1. Release planning (Release Calendar)
2. Prepare for build, test and deployment
3. Build and verify
4. Testing
5. Plan and prepare for production deployment

6. Perform production deployment
7. Verify production deployment
8. Early life cycle support
9. Review and close release

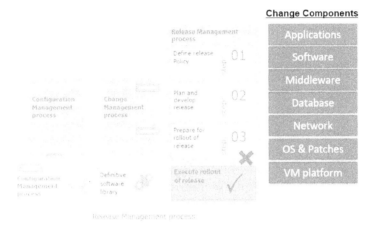

Figure 2.26: DevOps "Continuous Release Management" overview

2.1.33. DevOps "Continuous Release & Deployment Automation"

- **IBM UrbanCode** deploy provides an automation deployment framework that reduces deployment errors and improves efficiency, correctness, and traceability.
- **IBM UrbanCode** release orchestrates the *major release* ensuring multiple applications are successfully released.

Key Benefits:
- **Reduce errors:** Automated software release and deployment.
- **Improve productivity**: Push-button deployments for developer and operations.
- **Faster time-to-market:** Automated release and deployment with built-in best practices provides.
- **Compliance and auditability:** Enforced security and traceability.

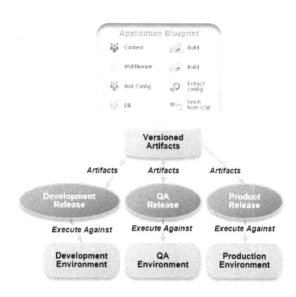

Figure 2.27: DevOps "Continuous Release & Deployment Automation" overview

2.1.34. DevOps "Capabilities" using "Quality Assurance"

The key automated *QA controls* within *DevOps Framework* can be focused through its *DevOps Tools* within its Continuous Delivery, Continuous Integration phase activities, as illustrated as follows:

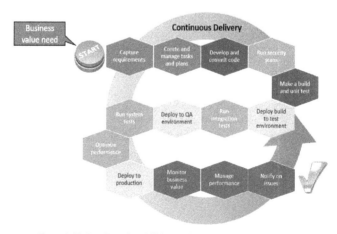

Figure 2.28: DevOps "Capabilities" using "Quality Assurance" overview

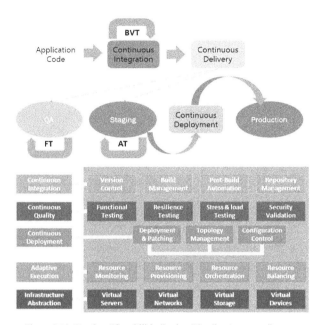

Figure 2.29: DevOps "Capabilities" using "Quality Assurance" process

2.1.35.   DevOps "Continuous Delivery" with in-built "Quality Assurance"

In a matured DevOps situation (Level-5), we can foresee QA built-in within each of DevOps focus phases/stages, thus ensuring quality checkpoint and integral to its next iterative phase or dependent activity.
Following screenshot, illustrates with the DevOps framework listing its phases of a project SDLC / application ALM, with its relation possible automation controls defined as per DevOps QA policy / principles.

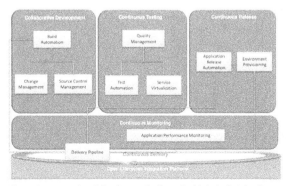

Figure 2.30: DevOps "Continuous Delivery" with in-built "Quality Assurance"

Continuous delivery flow

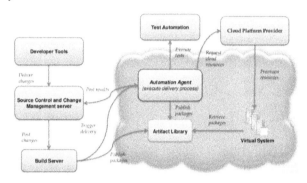

Figure 2.31: DevOps "Continuous Delivery" flow

2.1.36. DevOps "Capabilities" with in-built "Quality Assurance"

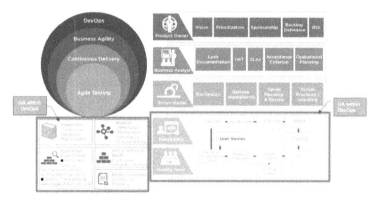

Figure 2.32: DevOps "Capabilities" with in-built "Quality Assurance"

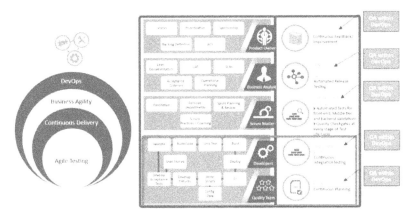

Figure 2.33: DevOps "Capabilities" with in-built "Quality Assurance" process overview

2.1.37. SDLC (Testing Phase): Testing Framework for Agile Projects, using DevOps Methods

E2E Testing, supported by DevOps accelerators & Continuous Improvements & Integrations.

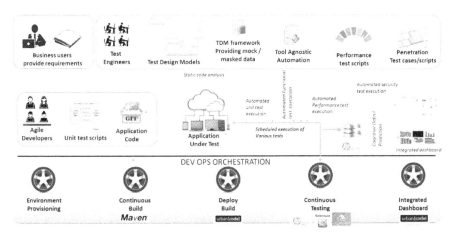

Figure 2.34: Testing Framework for Agile Projects, using DevOps Methods

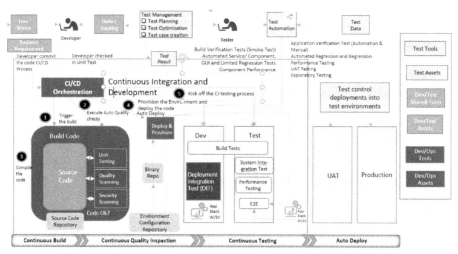

Figure 2.35: Testing Framework for Agile Projects, using DevOps Methods overview

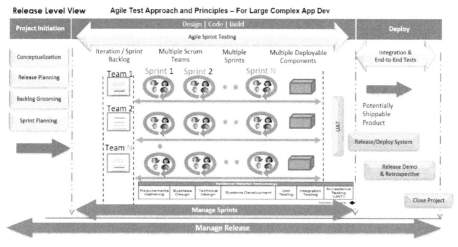

Figure 2.36: Agile Test Approach and Principles – For Large Complex App Dev

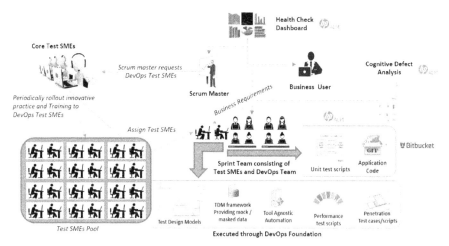

Figure 2.37: Testing Framework for Agile Projects, using DevOps Methods

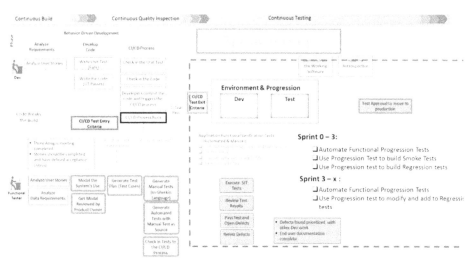

Figure 2.38: Testing Framework for Agile Projects, using DevOps Methods - Illustration

2.1.38. DevOps "Path to Production Model"

Illustrated view of *DevOps* tooling integration for *Path to Production* principle.

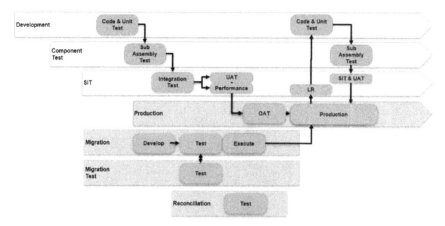

Figure 2.39: DevOps "Path to Production Model"

2.1.39. Process Comparisons – Traditional versus DevOps

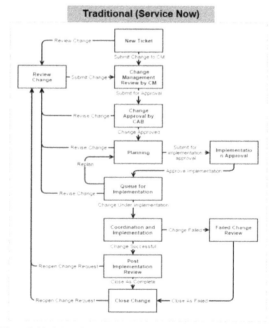

Figure 2.40: CHANGE Management: Traditional Process Overview (Standard Change)

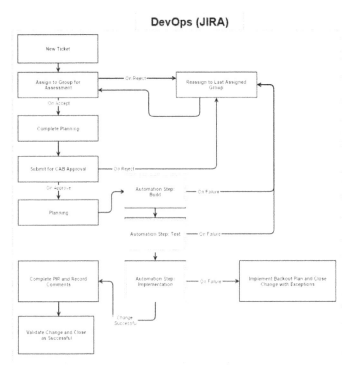

Figure 2.41: CHANGE Management: DevOps Process Overview (Standard Change)

2.1.40. Change Management Process Comparisons – Traditional versus DevOps

The following steps explain *normal* and DevOps change management process flow work:

Traditional	DevOps
When a ticket is raised, based on the matching conditions the entry criterion is verified to assign the request. By default, the request is assigned to *Change Management* group, when no conditions are matched.	When a change request is raised, based on the matching conditions, the entry criterion is verified to assign the request. When no conditions are matched, the request is assigned to *Change Management* group.
The *Change Coordinator* assesses and evaluates the request and submits the request for manager approval.	The *Release Coordination Group* assesses and evaluates the request. A plan is created to implement the request and assigned to **Change Advisory Board (CAB)** for approval.
The *Change Manager* performs one of the following actions on the request: • **Approve**: The request is assigned to the CAB for further assessment.	On approval by the CAB, the following steps are performed: • **Start Build Activity (Automated Script)**: Initiates the build script to create the software package for the release.

• **Reject**: The request is reassigned to the change coordinator for reevaluation or the request is cancelled/closed.	• **Check Build Status (Automated Script):** Verifies if the build script is running successfully. If the build fails, records the build and closes the request with exceptions. • **Start Test Activity (Automated Script):** Executes the test scripts to verify if the software package works as designed. • **Check Test Execution Status (Automated Script):** Verifies if the test is successful. If the test fails, run the back out plan or update the status as test failed and close the request with exceptions. • **Start Implementation (Release Automation):** Executes the deployment script to implement the package. • **Retrieve Release Status from Release Automation:** Gathers the release information from release automation application. **Note:** If the implementation fails, run the back out plan and close the request with exceptions.
The **CAB** assesses the request with one of the following actions: • **Approve by all approvers**:The request is approved by all the CAB members. • **Approve or reject by one approver**: The request is approved by one of the CAB members. • **Urgent approve by all approvers**: The request is submitted for an urgent approval by the CAB. **Note:** The Change Manager can withdraw the request from CAB approval and can close the request during approval phase.	The request is implemented and validated for completeness. The change request is then closed by the *Release Coordination Group*.
When the **CAB** approves, the change is approved for its implementation. If not, the CAB proposes an approval with modifications to the change request.	

Traditional

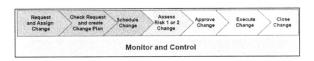

DevOps

Figure 2.42: CHANGE Management: Traditional vs DevOps Process Overview (Standard Change)

2.1.41. Quality Management Process Comparisons – Traditional vs DevOps

Quality Management: Traditional Framework

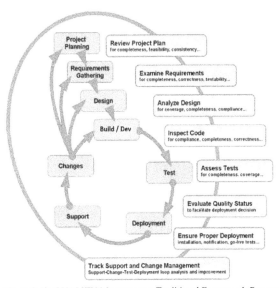

Figure 2.43: QUALITY Management: Traditional Framework Process flow

Traditional Method

- Qualitative checkpoint at every phase / level.
- Mostly manual intervention, based on baseline status.
- Automatic QA limited to *Build* and to some extent *Test* phases.
- QA through/using *Deliverables* quality approach & techniques.
- No direct integration between Development and Operations.
- Release, confirming final QA status/checkpoint (Success/Failure?).
- Sampled scenarios / projects, needing or confirming to QA status.
- QA by peer, teams, functions, clients (on their scope/phases).

Quality Management: Within DevOps Framework

Figure 2.44: QUALITY Assurance: Within / Using DevOps Framework

Within DevOps Framework

- Integral within SDLC and integrated to operations.
- Every phase confirms QA status/checkpoint (Success/Failure?).
- Automated controls for build, test and deploy lifecycles for IaaS, SaaS, PaaS.
- Automated configured QA checkpoint at every phase / level, while Deliverables QA is manually validated and certified.
- QA outcomes known, confirmed and validated between development and operations, with best automated controls.
- All scenarios and projects can easily confirm to QA status, with some exceptions of some projects on case-2-case (SaaS).
- *System QA* performed by configured automated systems and DevOps Tools, while *Manual QA* performed by teams & clients (on their scope/phases).

QUALITY Assurance: Within / Using DevOps Framework {Implementation Phase}

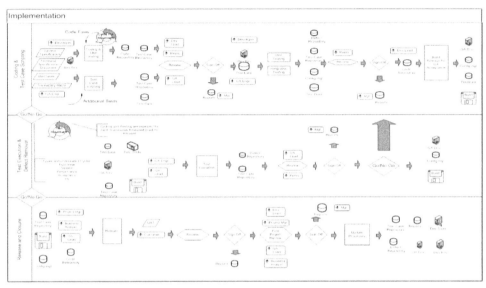

Figure 2.45: QUALITY Assurance: Using DevOps Framework - Implementation Phase

2.1.42.   Agile vs DevOps

Agile addresses gaps in *Customer* and *Developer* communications.

DevOps addresses gaps in Developer and IT Operations communications.

Agile	DevOps
Emphasizes breaking down barriers between developers and management / leadership.	Emphasizes breaking down barriers between software deployment teams and operation teams.
Addresses gaps between customer requirements and development teams.	Addresses gaps between development and operation teams.
Focuses more on functional and non-functional readiness.	Focuses more on operational and business readiness.
Agile development pertains mainly to the way development is thought out by the company.	Emphasizes on deploying software in the most reliable and safest ways which aren't necessarily always the fastest.
Agile development puts a huge emphasis on training all team members to have varieties of similar and equal skills. So that, when something went wrong, any team member can get assistance from any member in the absence of the team leader / SME / Architect.	DevOps, likes to divide and conquer, spreading the skill set between the development and operation teams. It also maintains consistent communication.
Agile development manages on *Sprints*. It means that the time table is much shorter (less than 30 days) and several features are to be produced and released in that period.	DevOps strives for consolidated deadlines and benchmarks with major releases, rather than smaller and more frequent ones

DevOps: Accelerating change delivery to achieve faster time to market.

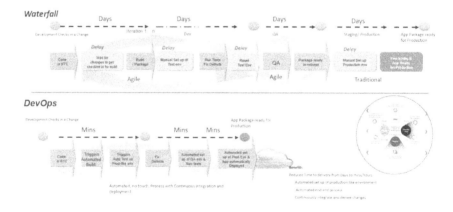

Figure 2.46: DevOps vs. Waterfall – Change Management

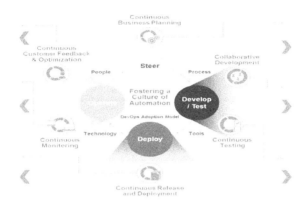

Figure 2.47: DevOps high level overview

2.1.43.   DevOps "Design Guiding Principles"

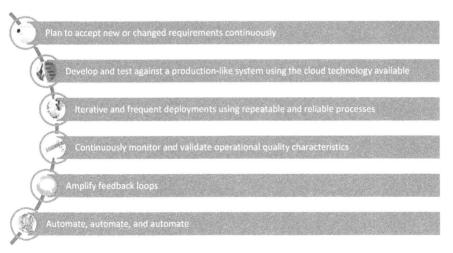

Figure 2.48: DevOps "Design Guiding Principles"

2.1.44. DevOps "Implementation Approach"

Analyze — Analyze each application for the SDLC pattern followed from requirement to release

Refine — Customize the Process framework to suit every applications' journey
Configure the applicable tools

On-board — Onboard every application for each of the identified DevOps practices
Fine Tune the toolchain as required to suit every application

Retrospect — Periodically review the progress to revise processes and tools configurations

Figure 2.49: DevOps "Implementation Approach"

2.1.45. DevOps "Implementation Considerations"

Content	Description
Implementation Strategy	• Once the applications are profiled for their SDLC behaviour pattern; a common set of processes, to be followed mandatorily by each of the application support team, will be defined. The tool chain may vary in future to accommodate any new application which may need a new compatible tool. • These processes will be aimed at facilitating continuous delivery objectives by adopting lean and Six Sigma principles and the necessary tools identified. Wherever required the necessary automation facilities will be availed from the vendor's cloud platform if available. • Each application has to be *on-boarded* for the continuous delivery mechanism to be followed by each and every member of the team

	ranging from the business to the IT support team which includes the vendors and the infrastructure teams as well.
	• The entire set of tools used in the SDLC will be supported by the PSI team for installation, configuration and day to day user support and maintenance.
Implementation Decisions & Waivers	• The following section lists the applicable implementation decisions and where agreed the waivers for existing decisions.
	• There are a number of solutions supplied by client vendors on either SaaS, PaaS, or IaaS model. The table in *Appendix C* lists the currently known classification of these applications. This classification may change as each of the application is studied for its detail software lifecycle.
	• Every application covered under the scope of the contract will be studied for deciding its lifecycle pattern and grouped together with other applications of similar nature. An entire set of processes and associated tools' usage to be followed for such applications will be documented. Such a document will form the application specific delivery from each of the system integrators.
	• Every business application will need to have mandatorily go through the Business planning and release management practices.
	• The DevOps CI, CD, and CT practices will be evaluated and implemented on a case to case basis for each of the applications.
	• All recommended DevOps tools are available in private environment hosted in cloud and should be used for supporting the On-premise and IaaS applications.
	• Any applications hosted in a SaaS environment may be expected to use the tools and processes recommended by the SaaS vendor.

2.1.46.   DevOps Modelling "per Product Types"

Every IT System (Product/Application) project delivery goes through *Software Delivery Life Cycle* which consists of following stages:
- Business Planning
- Business & IT Requirements
- Analysis & Design
- Development
- Unit Testing
- Deployment (in various staging environments)
- Testing for functionality and NFRs
- Release Management
- Monitoring (applications and user satisfaction)

On-Premise	IaaS	PaaS	SaaS
Application	Application	Application	Application
Data	Data	Data	Data
Runtime	Runtime	Runtime	Runtime
Middleware	Middleware	Middleware	Middleware
OS	OS	OS	OS
Virtualization	Virtualization	Virtualization	Virtualization
Servers	Servers	Servers	Servers
Storage	Storage	Storage	Storage
Networking	Networking	Networking	Networking

Component can be configured within DevOps

Component managed by and within Vendor network

Figure 2.50: DevOps Modelling "per Product Types"

XaaS Type	Definition	Examples
On-Premise	*Custom Design-developed* applications using a high level language.	
IaaS	**Infrastructure-as-a-Service (IaaS)** is a form of cloud computing that provides virtualized computing resources over the Internet. It's highly standardized selective computing functionality – such as compute power, storage, archive or other basic infrastructure components.	Cisco Metapod, Microsoft Azure, **Amazon Web Services** (**AWS**).
PaaS	**Platform-as-a-Service (PaaS)** is a category of cloud computing services that provides a platform allowing *customers to develop*, *run*, *and manage applications* without the complexity of building and maintaining the infrastructure typically associated with developing and launching an *app*.	Azure, AT&T, Netsuite, Google App Engine, Force.com
SaaS	**Software-as-a-Service (SaaS)** is a software licensing and delivery model, in which software is licensed on a subscription basis and is centrally hosted. SaaS is typically accessed by users, using a thin client via a web browser.	Google Apps, Salesforce, Citrix Cisco WebEx, Office Live

2.1.47. DevOps "Capability Modelling per XaaS Types Components"

Table below illustrates with analysis of *DevOps Capabilities* per XaaS categories / types.
Each DevOps Capability, per XaaS type should be considered based on each component scope.

DevOps "Capabilities"	On-Premise	IaaS	PaaS	SaaS
Continuous Business Planning	Yes	Yes	Yes	Yes
Continuous Integration (CI)	Yes	Yes	Yes	No
Continuous Testing (CT)	Yes	Yes	Yes	Depends
Continuous Deployment (CD)	Yes	Yes	Yes	Depends
Continuous Environment Provisioning (CE)	Depends	Yes	Depends	Depends
Continuous Release Management (CR)	Yes	Yes	Yes	Yes
Continuous Monitoring (CM)	Yes	Yes	Yes	Yes
Continuous Optimization & User Feedback	Yes	Yes	Yes	Yes

Figure 2.51: DevOps "Capability Modelling per XaaS Types Components"

2.1.48. DevOps "Tools Modelling Solution"

Sr. No.	Component	Definition	Proposed Tools Suite
1	Collaborative Development	Enables team communication and integrates with DevOps tools for in context discussions.	Confluence
2	Requirements & Design	Business process reengineering	IBM Rational DOORS, IBM Blueworks Live, EA Sparx
3	Track & Plan	Work items effective tracking	HP Octane
4	Development	Enables developers to write source code usually with a developer environment.	Eclipse, Atom, Sublime Text, Swagger, etc.
5	Source Control	Source code management and versioning.	Git-Bitbucket

6	**Build**	Compile, Package, Unit-test, and preparation of software assets.	Maven
7	**Test**	Integration test, UFT, NFT, Performance test.	HP ALM, HP UFT, HP Performance Center, Blazemeter, Selenium, BrowserStack, Rapit, Cyara, CA LISA, CA TDM
8	**Continuous Integration**	A part of DevOps capability model.	Jenkins
9	**Artefact Management**	Management of the output from the build.	IBM UrbanCode Deploy
10	**Release Management**	Enables management, preparation and deployment of releases	HP Octane, IBM UrbanCode Release
11	**Deployment Orchestration**	Processes required to get the Release into Production Env.	IBM UrbanCode Deploy
12	**IT Cloud Orchestration**		IBM UrbanCode Deploy, Blue Print Designer/ Heat Engine
13	**Configuration Management**	Automatic provision of new SCM CI's (not CMDB CI's).	IBM UrbanCode Deploy, Blue Print Designer/ Heat Engine
14	**Issue Management**	Program level issues/risk management.	HP Octane ALM

2.1.49.   DevOps Capabilities Model within "SDLC Framework"

SDLC "DevOps Framework"	DevOps "Capabilities"	Participants "To engage for Design & Implement"
Continuous Business Planning (CP)	• Capture business requirements	Business, IT managers, Vendor managers Business, IT managers, Vendor

	• Analyse business requirements • Prioritize business requirements • Project Planning • Measure to Project Metrics • Requirements Traceability • Dashboard portfolio measures	managers Audit, Program managers Domain Program Managers Everybody (role specific dashboards)
Collaborative Development (CD)	Release Planning Collaborative Development Configuration Management Build Management Change Management Dashboards Requirements Traceability	Business, IT managers, Vendor managers Architects, Business analysts, Developers, Test professionals Developers Developers IT managers, Vendor managers Everybody Project managers, developers, testers
Continuous Testing (CT)	Test Management and execution Test Automation Test Data Management	Program Managers, Test Managers Testers Testers, Business Analysts
Continuous Release and Deployment (CD)	Release Management Environment Management (Provisioning automation) Deployment Automation (Application, Middleware and DBs)	Domain Program Managers, Release managers Test managers, Deployment / Release managers Service & Domain Operations managers
Continuous Monitoring (CM)	Monitor Capacity and Optimize Monitor Performance and Optimize Monitor User Experience and Optimize Event and Incident Management Operational Analytics	Service & Domain Operations managers Service & Domain Operations managers Client Business managers Service & Domain Operations managers Service & Domain Operations managers

2.1.50. DevOps – Case Study 1

Facebook Dark Launching Technique

Dark launching is the process of *gradually rolling out production-ready features* to a select set of users before a full release. This allows development teams to get user *feedback early on, test bugs, and also stress test* infrastructure performance. A direct result of continuous delivery, this method of release helps in *faster, more iterative releases* that ensure that application performance does not get affected and that the release is well received by customers.

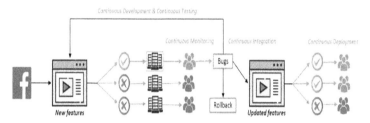

Figure 2.50: Facebook Dark Launching Technique

DEMO Application

Login use case implementation

Figure 2.51: Valid user log in

Tools and Technologies used
- Servlets/JSP using Eclipse IDE
- Tomcat as servlet container
- Git/GitHub for source code and version control repository
- Jenkins for continuous integration and delivery

- Maven for build
- Jenkins plugins
- TestNG, Selenium and Junit for unit testing
- PMD/Checkstyle for source code validation
- CatLight for monitor Jenkins job status and show notifications

Git/GitHub Repository

Figure 2.52: Git/GitHub Repository overview

Jenkins dashboard

Figure 2.53: Jenkins dashboard overview

Delivery pipeline

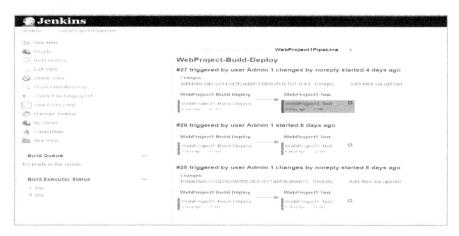

Figure 2.54: Delivery pipeline overview

Automated emails

- **Build confirmation**

Figure 2.55: Build confirmation

- **Build failure**

Figure 2.56: Build failure

Test execution report

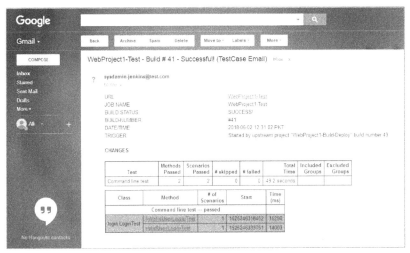

Figure 2.57: Test execution report

2.1.51. DevOps – Case Study 2

GE

The challenge

- GE Power Fleet Services development and production teams had faced an obstacle in their endeavor towards continuous improvement.

- They wanted to develop higher quality software faster, and enhance collaboration between development and production.

Requirements

- Normalize, accelerate, and automate deployments to Dev, Test, Staging, and Production environments

- Arrange, manage, and standardize release pipelines across all tools in the environment

- Build once, deploy many

- Collect release details

- Visualize the release data for stakeholders

- Build on their Continuous Integration foundation

Solution

GE Power chose the DevOps platform to automate their deployments and to compose and control their release pipelines.

Results

- Releases that took months, now take days and only 1/3 of the resources

- Higher quality software

- Removal of rework increased capacity to innovate, which improved revenue growth

- Saved 25 hours per deployment

- Critical release data helps team make quick, data-driven decisions, and measure success

- Alleviation from legacy process to release automation was accelerated

2.1.52.   Appendix – Backup / References

The Leadership Suite DevOps and Business Alignment Success Guide:
https://devops.com/6-blogs-for-devops-business-alignment/

DevOps Viewpoints from Pink17:

https://devops.com/devops-viewpoints-pink17/

10 Must Read DevOps Articles to Stay in the Know:

https://www.actifio.com/company/blog/post/10-must-read-devops-articles-to-stay-in-the-know-for-2016/

5 Things DevOps is Not:

https://devops.com/what-devops-is-not/

Version Control & Code Review – SAP:

http://docs.abapgit.org/
https://github.com/larshp/abapGit

Continuous Delivery & Build – SAP:

https://medium.com/pacroy/continuous-integration-in-abap-3db48fc21028

SLACK Integration with Jenkins

https://wiki.jenkins.io/display/JENKINS/Slack+Plugin

http://www.maheshchikane.com/how-to-jenkins-build-n-deploy-slack-jenkins-integration-2/

https://stackoverflow.com/questions/30272541/jenkins-slack-integration

https://archive.sap.com/discussions/thread/3834623

https://blogs.sap.com/2015/12/13/want-to-use-bitbucket-as-your-project-repository-with-sap-web-ide/

2.1.53. Glossary

Acronym	Definition
ALM	Application Lifecycle Management
CI	Configuration Item *(related to SCM or & CMDB process)*
CI	Continuous Integration, *(a DevOps capability)*
CD	Continuous Deployment, *(a DevOps capability)*
CT	Continuous Testing, *(a DevOps capability)*
CM	Continuous Monitoring, *(a DevOps capability)*

CP	Continuous Planning, *(a DevOps capability)*
CMDB	Configuration Management Database, *(relates/refers to "Asset Management")*
CHG	Change ID, *(relates to Change management process)*
CAB	Change Advisory Board, *(relates to Change management process)*
DEV	Relates or refers to "Development"
QA	Quality Assurance
REL	Release Management Process
RFC	Request for Change
SDLC	Software Development Lifecycle
SCM	Software Configuration Management
TEST	Relates or refers to "Testing"
QC	Quality Control
QA	Quality Assurance

Figure 2.58: Terms & Acronyms

2.1.54. DevOps – Key Takeaways

DevOps is a cultural movement based on human and technical interactions to improve relationships and results.

DevOps is not a goal, but a never ending process of continual improvement.

--Jez Humble

What is the DevOps model?
- Integration of teams working on fixing defects and implementing change requests.

Why are we moving to DevOps model?
- Choice of prioritisation of business needs
- Increased velocity in delivering changes

- Efficiency benefits in having one team responsible for both sustain and change services
- Continuous delivery

What changes from a user perspective?
- Single queue in myIT
- Work driven by business priority (no longer SLA timelines)
- Approved change requests stay open until they are implemented
- Better transparency of where items are in the queue

What stays the same?

• DevOps requires a cultural change to improve quality and reliability.
• There are many constantly changing technical challenges facing DevOps.
• There are a number of categories of software tools, each with a number of choices.
• Cloud computing eliminates the need for expensive data centers and supporting groups.
• Information security is important to protect sensitive assets.
• Architecture is structure that defines how systems communicate and work together.
• It is important to ensure that requirements are complete and consistent.
• User acceptance test are essential to ensure that all functional requirements have been correctly implemented.

Some facts

• According to *Puppet Lab's 2015 State of DevOps Report*, "High-performing IT organizations experience 60 times fewer failures and recover from failure 168 times faster than their lower-performing peers. They also deploy 30 times more frequently with 200 times shorter lead times."

• A **Forrester report** titled *The New Software Imperative: Fast Delivery With Quality* found that *development teams that consistently deliver at the fastest cycle times enjoy the highest business satisfaction*. Importantly, teams that were able to deliver new applications the fastest were also creating the highest-quality software.

At Google:
• 15000+ engineers working on 4000+ projects
• 5500 code commits/day
• 75 million test cases are run daily
• 10 deploys per day Dev & Ops cooperation at Flickr
• Amazon deploys every 11 second on an average
• 30x more frequent deployment
• 2x the change success rate
• 12x faster Mean Time To Recover (MTTR)
• 2x more likely to exceed profitability market share & productivity goals
• 50% higher market capitalization growth over 3 years

Top predictors of IT performance

- Version control of all production artifacts
- Automated acceptance testing
- Continuous Integration & Continuous Deployment
- Peer review of production changes
- High trust culture
- Proactive monitoring of the production environment
- Win-Win relations between Dev & Ops

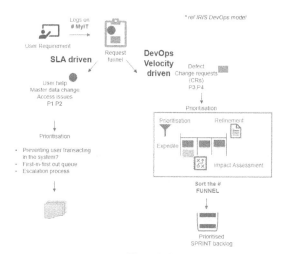

Figure 2.59: DevOps model

2.1.55. What are DevOps Goals?

- Produce smaller, more frequent software releases
- Reduce effort and risks associated with software development, transition and operation
- Improve time to market
- Better align IT responsiveness and capabilities to business needs
- Produce smaller, more frequent software releases
- Reduce effort and risks associated with software development, transition, and operation
- Improve time to market
- Improve quality of code
- Improve quality of software deployments
- Reduce cost of product iterations and delays
- Instill a culture of communication and collaboration
- Improve productivity
- Improve visibility into IT requirements and processes

2.1.56. What are important DevOps Tools used in JAVA and in SAP?

Sr. No.(s)	Phases(s)	Tool(s) JAVA	Tool(s) SAP / Cloud S/4 HANA
1	**Continuous Integration (CI)**	Jenkins	Jenkins
2	**Continuous Release and Deployment (CD)**	Jenkins	Jenkins
3	Continuous delivery and build	GIT HUB / Maven	abapGit, SCII, SLIN, ST05, SE30, ABAP Unit Code Coverage
4	Configuration management	SaltStack / Ansible, JIRA	SQA, JIRA
5	Continuous testing	HP ALM / Selenium Testing	HP ALM / Selenium Testing
6	Version control and Code review	GitLab	abapGit

2.1.57. What are 6Cs and 25 Principles of DevOps?

6Cs and 25 Principles of DevOps

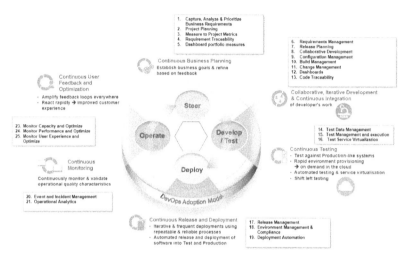

Figure 2.60: 6Cs and 25 Principles of DevOps

2.1.58.   Explain one DevOps toolsets through SAP lifecycle?

DevOps toolset through lifecycle (an example – primarily SAP portfolio)

Figure 2.61: DevOps toolsets

2.1.59.   Explain DevOps estimation?

DevOps estimation

Estimation Methodology

Technical Sizing

Size	Complexity	DevOps Rating	No of Story Points
Small	Simple	1	1
Medium	Simple	2	2
Small	Intermediate	3	3
Large	Simple	4	5
Medium	Intermediate	5	8
Small	High	6	13
Large	Intermediate	7	21
Medium	High	8	34
Large	High	9	55

9 Box Estimation Model for DevOps sizing

	1	2	3
SMALL	1	2	3
	0.9	1.7	2.6
	4	5	6
Medium	5	8	13
	4.3	6.9	11.3
	7	8	9
Large	21	34	55
	18.2	29.5	47.7

Box #
Story Point
Effort (MD)

Figure 2.62: DevOps Estimation

2.1.60. Explain DevOps sample Project Plan?

30 -60 -90 Day DevOps Plan

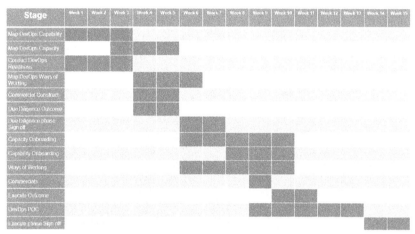

Figure 2.63: DevOps Project Plan – Example 1

2.1.61.   Explain one sample DevOps meeting charter?

DevOps meeting charter

The following table presents the initial weekly schedule of DevOps activities. The Sprint duration is 2 weeks.

Activity	Participants	Time	Monday	Tuesday	Wednesday	Thursday	Friday
Triage	Virtual Team		x	x	x	x	x
Daily Stand Up	Scrum Team		x	x	x	x	x
Backlog Prioritisation	Product Owner Product Advisor Scrum Master		x				
Sprint Demo**	Scrum Teams Product Owner (Optional)			x			
Sprint Planning* & Retrospective**	Scrum Team Product Owner			x			
Change Review Board	CRB Team				x		
CRB LT Response	Leadership Team	Email					x

Figure 2.64: DevOps meeting charter – Example 1

2.1.62. Explain one sample DevOps Change review board team role and responsibilities?

Change review board Team - weekly

Change Review board	Key role
Product Owner	Agrees or assigns new business value prioritisation and approves or rejects change request
Product Advisors	Provide input to product owner regarding business value, solution context, existing user stories Take ownership of ticket and respond to user
Scrum Master	Provide technical inputs
SME	Consulted offline

2.1.63. Explain one sample ABAP development process?

SAP Technology stack – ABAP Development Process

Automate unit testing to verify that when code is created or changed it behaves as intended and that anything using that code will work properly as long as the unit test is passed. Tools like ABAP Unit can be used to develop and build unit tests within an SAP environment. Ideally, these tests should be executed automatically before transports are released, so the code can be verified before being moved anywhere.

Figure 2.65: SAP development process

2.1.64.   Explain DevOps Values?

DevOps is a cultural movement based on human and technical interactions to improve relationships and results.

Figure 2.66: DevOps Values - CAMS

2.1.65.   Explain characteristics of DevOps Culture?

* Shared vision, goals and incentives
* Open, honest, two-way communication
* Collaboration
* Pride of workmanship
* Respect
* Trust
* Transparency
* Continuous improvement
  – Experimentation
  – Intelligent risk taking
  – Learning
  – Practicing

* Data-driven
* Safe
* Reflection
* Recognition

2.1.66.   Explain automation enablers in DevOps?

* Treating infrastructure as code
* Repeatable and reliable deployment processes: CI/CD
* Development and testing performed against production-like systems
* On-demand creation of development, test, staging, and production environments
* Proactive monitoring of infrastructure components, environments, systems and services.

DevOps is not just about automation but there are common enabling practices.

2.1.67. What do you mean by CI/CD in DevOps?

Continuous Integration

•Integrate the code change by each developer and run test cases

Continuous Delivery

•Taking each CI build and run it through deployment procedures on test and staging environment, so that it's ready to be deployed in production anytime.

Continuous Deployment
Continuous deployment is the next step of continuous delivery: Every change that passes the automated tests is deployed to production automatically.

Figure 2.67: DevOps – Continuous delivery and continuous deployment

2.1.68. What you can automate in DevOps?

• Builds
• Deployments
• Tests
• Monitoring
• Self-healing
• System rollouts
• System configuration

2.1.69. What do you mean by high level DevOps Lifecycle?

•**Before - pre development**

Do business process reengineering to identify the functional requirements and non-functional requirements from customer perspectives.

- Security
- Backup
- Availability
- Upgradability
- Configuration management
- Monitoring
- Logging
- Metrics

- **During**

  - Communication
  - Source control
  - Automate builds
  - Automate tests
  - Automate deployments (Dev, QA, Prod)
  - System metrics

- **After - post deployment**

- Release
  - Monitor applications and systems/servers
  - Continue to run tests
  - Retrospective meetings

- Issues (yes, they do happen)
  - Post mortem

2.1.70.   Can DevOps be Standalone?

No.

DevOps cannot be standalone.

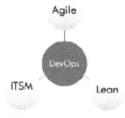

Successful DevOps relies on the adoption and integration of multiple frameworks and methodologies.

Figure 2.68: DevOps – Integration with Agile, Lean and ITSM

2.1.71. How can DevOps increase the Agility?

DevOps extends agile principles beyond the boundaries of the software to the entire delivered service.

DevOps increases agility by:

• Breaking down silos
• Improving constraints
• Taking a unified approach to systems engineering
• Applying agile principles to both Dev and Ops
• Sharing knowledge, skills, experience, and data
• Recognizing the criticality of automation
• Deploying faster with fewer errors

2.1.72. Does DevOps and Lean work together in an organization?

Yes, improving the flow of work between Dev and Ops will remove many types of waste.

2.1.73. Does DevOps and ITSM work together in an organization?

Yes, all ITSM processes will ultimately play a role in supporting DevOps by increasing flow, reducing constraints and creating business value.

Key ITSM processes that help enable DevOps include:

• Change Management
• Release and Deployment Management
• Service Asset and Configuration Management
• Knowledge Management
• Problem Management
• Incident Management
• Event Management

2.1.74. What are the desired skills in DevOps?

It may be like the following:

Desired Skills	Percentage (%)
Coding or scripting	84%
People skills – good communication and collaboration skills	60%
Business Process Reengineering skills (using Agile, Lean, ITSM)	56%
Experience with devops specific skills	19%

2.1.75.   Who is DevOps Engineer?

• Currently there is no job role skill sets for a DevOps Engineer.

  These roles may be filled by:
– Developers interested in deployment
– System Administrators who enjoy scripting and coding

• General characteristics include someone who:
– Can contribute / add values to business and process improvement initiatives
– Is a good collaborator
– Wants to be in a shared culture promoting workplace

2.1.76.   Where to begin DevOps automation?

• Simplify first – don't automate bad processes
• Automate high value and repetitive tasks
• Automate error-prone work
• Automate to optimize workflow bottlenecks and communication flows
• Improve automated monitoring and notification practices, make it easy for people to do the right thing!

"Your tools alone will not make you successful."
                                    --Patrick Debois

2.1.77.   Explain precisely JIRA Software?

JIRA is a web-based open source licensed *Issue tracking system* or *Bug tracking system*. It is mainly used for agile project management. JIRA is a proprietary based tool, developed by Atlassian (www.atlassian.com). The product name 'JIRA' is shortened from the word *Gojira*, which means Godzilla in Japanese. JIRA helps us to manage the project effectively and smoothly. It is a powerful tool to track the issues, bugs, backlogs of the project. It helps the team to strive hard towards the common goal. JIRA is widely used by many organizations across the world.

Key Features of JIRA Includes:

  a. Scrum boards
  b. Project planning
  c. Project tracking
  d. Reporting
  e. Notifications

Advantages of JIRA

  - Improves collaboration
  - Improves tracking
  - Better planning
  - Increase productivity

- Improves customer satisfaction
- Flexible to use

2.1.78. Explain precisely Jenkins Software?

Jenkins is a DevOps tool for doing continuous integration and continuous delivery. For monitoring executions of repeated jobs this tool can be used. It has 100 plus plugins. Via a web interface this tool can be easily set up and can be configured. To integrate project changes more easily and access outputs for quickly identifying problems, this tool can be used.

Key Features:
• Self-contained Java-based program
• Continuous integration and continuous delivery
• Via a web interface it can be easily set up and configured
• It has more than 100 plugins
• For monitoring executions of repeated jobs this tool can be used

2.1.79. Explain precisely Docker?

An integrated technology suite enabling DevOps teams to build, ship, and run distributed applications anywhere, Docker is a tool that allows users to quickly assemble applications from components and work collaboratively. This open platform for distributed applications is appropriate for managing containers of an app as a single group and clustering an app's containers to optimize resources and provide high availability.

Key Features:

• Package dependencies with your applications in Docker containers to make them portable and predictable during development, testing, and deployment
• Works with any stack
• Isolates applications in containers to eliminate conflicts and enhance security
• Streamline DevOps collaboration to get features and fixes into production more quickly

2.1.80. Explain precisely Vagrant?

It is a DevOps Tool. To create / configure portable, lightweight, and reproducible development environments, this tool can be used. It has easy to use workflows. It focuses on automation. While setting up development environments, this tool saves DevOps teams time.

Key Features:
• No complicated setup process; on Mac OS X, Windows, or a popular distribution of Linux, just download and install it within few minutes.
• To create / configure portable, lightweight, and reproducible development environments, this tool can be used.
• While setting up development environments, this tool saves DevOps teams time.

2.1.81. Explain precisely Puppet?

It is a DevOps tool. It can be used for continuous delivery. It helps to deploy changes quickly with confidence / release better software. By decreasing cycle times, it helps to increase reliability. It helps team to become *being agile* and pays keen attention to customer needs in an automated testing environment. It ensures consistency across different boxes (like, DEV, TEST, PROD).

2.1.82. Explain precisely Chef?

It is a DevOps tool. It can be used for achieving speed, scale, and consistency by automating your infrastructure. It helps users to quickly respond to changing customer needs.

Key Features:
• Accelerate cloud adoption
• Manage data center and cloud environments
• Manage multiple cloud environments
• Maintain high availability

2.1.83. Explain precisely Ansible?

It is a DevOps tool. It can be used to speed productivity and to effectively manage complex deployments by automating the entire application lifecycle.

Key Features:

• Deploy applications
• Manage systems
• Avoid complexity
• Simple IT automation that eliminates repetitive tasks and frees teams to do more strategic work

2.1.84. Explain precisely Salt Stack?

It is a DevOps tool. It can be used for configuration management at scale. It can manage heterogeneous computing environments and can orchestrate any cloud. It can automate unique infrastructure / deployment of nearly any infrastructure and application stack used to create modern cloud, enterprise IT, and web-scale.

2.1.85. Explain precisely Visual Studio IDE?

It is a DevOps tool. It can be used for writing code accurately and efficiently while retaining the current file context in development environment for Android, iOS, web, and cloud. It can be used to refactor, identify and fix code issues. It can be used to easily zoom into details like call structure, related functions and test status. It can be used to easily develop and deploy SQL Server / Azure SQL databases with ease.

2.1.86.   Explain precisely Nagios?

It is a DevOps tool. It can be used for monitoring IT infrastructure components such as applications, network infrastructure, system metrics and so on. It helps in searching log data.

2.1.87.   Explain precisely RabbitMQ?

An open source multi-protocol messaging broker, RabbitMQ is a DevOps tool that supports a large number of developer platforms. RabbitMQ also runs on almost all operating systems and is easy to use.

Key Features:

• Enables software applications to connect and scale
• Gives applications a common platform for sending and reaching messages and provides a safe place for messages to sit until received
• Flexible routing, reliability, clustering, highly available queues, and more

2.1.88.   Explain precisely SolarWinds Log & Event Manager?

SolarWinds offers IT management software and monitoring tools. It can be used for providing solution for security, compliance, and troubleshooting.

Key Features:

• Normalize logs to quickly identify security incidents and simplify troubleshooting
• Out-Of-The-Box rules and reports for easily meeting industry compliance requirements
• Node-based licensing
• Real-time event correlation
• Real-time remediation
• File integrity monitoring
• Licenses for 30 nodes to 2,500 nodes

2.1.89.   Explain precisely Prometheus?

It is a DevOps tool. It can be used for monitoring system and time series database. Its alert system can handle notifications and silencing. It can support more than 10 languages and includes easy-to-implement custom libraries. It is popular with teams using Grafana.

2.1.90. Explain precisely Ganglia?

Ganglia provides DevOps teams with cluster and grid monitoring capabilities. This scalable tool is designed for high-performance computing systems like clusters and grids. Ganglia makes use of XML, XDR, and RRD tools.

Key Features:

• Scalable distributed monitoring system based on a hierarchical design targeted at federations of clusters
• Achieves low per-node overheads for high concurrency
• Can scale to handle clusters with 2,000 nodes

2.1.91. Explain precisely Splunk?

It is a DevOps tool. It can be used for delivering operational intelligence to teams. It can help companies to gain more security and productivity in competitive market.
It helps in delivering a central, unified view of IT services. It helps in next-generation monitoring and analytics solution. It can adapt thresholds dynamically, can highlight discrepancies and can detect areas of impact.

2.1.92. Explain precisely Sumo Logic?

Sumo Logic helps leading companies analyze and make sense of log data. DevOps teams choose Sumo Logic because it combines security analytics with integrated threat intelligence for advanced security analytics with deep insights for modern applications.

Key Features:

• Build, run, and secure AWS, Azure, or Hybrid applications
• Cloud-native, machine data analytics service for log management and time series metrics
• One platform for real-time continuous intelligence
• Remove friction from your application lifecycle

2.1.93. Explain precisely Log Stash?

It is a DevOps tool. It can be used for server side of data processing and it can dynamically transform & prepare data no matter its format or complexity. It can collect, parse, and transform logs. Here, pipelines are multipurpose and may be sophisticated to give you full visibility when monitoring deployments or even an active Logstash node.

2.1.94. Explain precisely Loggly?

It is a DevOps tool. It can be used to simplify cloud log management and for quick & efficient resolution of operational issues. It can be used to enhance customer delight by delivering good quality code of deliverables. It may use open protocols rather than proprietary agents to send logs. It can provide effective solutions helping businesses access, manage and analyze log data across the entire application stack on AWS.

2.1.95. Explain precisely Paper trail?

It is a DevOps tool. It can be used for instant log visibility and to realize value from logs you already collect. It can be used to tail & search using a browser, command-line, or API. It can be used to aggregate (all app logs, logfiles, and syslog in one place). It can also be used to react and analyze (get instant alerts, detect trends, and archive forever).

2.1.96. Explain precisely Apache ActiveMQ?

It is a DevOps tool. It can be used for high-performance clustering, client-server, peer-based communication. It is fast, and fully supports JMS 1.1 and J2EE 1.4. It can support several cross language clients and protocols.
It can be easily embedded into Spring applications. It can be configured using Spring's XML configuration mechanism. It supports advanced features like message groups, virtual destinations, wildcards, and composite destinations.

2.1.97. Explain precisely Squid?

As a cache proxy for the web, Squid is a DevOps tool which optimizes web delivery and supports HTTP, HTTPS, FPT, and more. By reducing bandwidth and improving response times via caching and reusing frequently-requested web pages, Squid also operates as a server accelerator.

Key Features:

• Extensive access controls
• Runs on most available operating systems including Windows
• Licensed under the GNU GPL
• Improves performance by optimizing data flow between client & server
• Caches frequently-used content to save bandwidth.

2.1.98. Explain precisely MCollective @Puppetize?

It is a DevOps tool, it is useful while teams are working with large number of servers or working with parallel job execution systems or involved in building orchestration in server. It can use a rich data source, can perform real time discovery across the network.

2.1.99. Explain precisely CF Engine?

CF Engine helps us to do configuration management. This tool is very much helpful to automate large scale complex infrastructure. It is written in C. It is an open source configuration solution.
A DevOps tool for IT automation at web scale, CF Engine is ideal for configuration management and helps teams automate large-scale, complex, and mission-critical infrastructure. With CF Engine, you can ensure compliance even while securely making consistent global changes. It is scalable.

2.1.100.   Explain precisely Gradle?

Delivering adaptable, fast automation for teams using DevOps, it accelerates productivity of developer. It helps DevOps team to deliver faster, better, cheaper Software deliverables. Developer can code in any languages here, like, Python, C++, JAVA. It has rich API and many plugins.

Key Features:

• It accelerates productivity of developer.
• It helps DevOps team to deliver faster, better, cheaper Software deliverables.
• It has rich API and many plugins.
• Developer can code in any languages here, like Python, C++, JAVA.

2.1.101.   Explain precisely Jfrog Artifactory?

JFrog is enterprise-ready repository manager. It is language independent as well as technology independent.
It can be integrated with all major DevOps and CI/CD tools. It can be used for end to end tracking of artifacts from development till production.

Key Features:

• Enterprise-ready repository manager
• It can be integrated with all major DevOps and CI/CD tools. It can be used for end to end tracking of artifacts from development till production

2.1.102.   Explain precisely Pros and Cons of Puppet?

Pros:

• Well-established support community through Puppet Labs
• It has the most mature interface and runs on nearly every OS
• Simple installation and initial setup
• Most complete Web UI in this space
• Strong reporting capabilities

Cons:

• For more advanced tasks, you will need to use the CLI, which is Ruby-based (meaning you'll have to understand Ruby).

• Support for pure-Ruby versions (rather than those using Puppet's customized DSL) is being scaled back.
• Because of the DSL and a design that does not focus on simplicity, the Puppet code base can grow large, unwieldy, and hard to pick up for new people in your organization at higher scale.
• Model-driven approach means less control compared to code-driven approaches.

2.1.103. Explain precisely Pros and Cons of Chef?

Pros:

• Rich collection of modules and configuration recipes.
• Code-driven approach gives you more control and flexibility over your configurations.
• Being centered around Git gives it strong version control capabilities.
• *Knife* tool (which uses SSH for deploying agents from workstation) eases installation burdens.

Cons:

• Learning curve is steep if you're not already familiar with Ruby and procedural coding.
• It's not a simple tool, which can lead to large code bases and complicated environments.
• It doesn't support push functionality.

2.1.104. Explain DevOps Best Practices – Tools perspective?

•Automated testing
•Integrated Configuration Management
•Integrated Change Management
•Continuous Integration
•Continuous Deployment
•Application Monitoring
•Automated Dashboards

2.1.105. Explain DevOps Best Practices – high level?

• Break Silos in IT
• Adjust performance reviews
• Create real-time visibility
• Use software automation wherever you can
• Choose tools that are compatible with each other
• Start with pilot projects
• Continuously deploy applications
• Create a service environment within the company
• Understand the collaboration and shared tools strategy for the Dev, QA, and infrastructure automation teams
• Use tools to capture any request
• Use agile kanban project management for automation and devops requests that can be dealt with in the tooling
• Use tools to log metrics on both manual and automated processes

• Implement test automation and test data provisioning tools
• Perform acceptance test for each deployment tooling
• Ensure continuous feedback between the teams to spot gaps, issues, and inefficiencies
• Build the right culture and keep the momentum going: Once you start your DevOps process, continue to improve and refine it
• Focus on culture not the tools
• Conduct version control and automation
• Create tight feedback loops
• Participate in DevOps Community
• Redefine your skill sets: The most salient skills their respondents say they look for in hiring for their DevOps teams are coding and scripting (84%), people skills (60%), process re-engineering skills (56%) and then experience with specific tools (19%).

2.1.106. Explain DevOps in a Nutshell?

For most enterprises, increasing the speed of deployment is a key goal of their DevOps initiatives. In order to achieve that goal, they often deploy technology that promises to speed development and they frequently implement Agile development techniques, such as test-driven development, continuous integration, pair programming, and Scrum methodologies. Experts say it's important for organizations to remember that the techniques and the technology aren't the goal in themselves; instead, they are a means for accomplishing goals like faster deployment, improved code quality and, ultimately, better support for the business.

2.1.107. Explain DevOps flow in a Nutshell?

• Create issue in Jira
• Commit changes to Bitbucket
• Code is pushed to Gerrit
• Code review done
• Gerrit pushes to Bitbucket
• Jenkins checks out, compile, package, run unit test
• Jenkins create docker image and deploys container to QA server
• Jenkins pushes image to registry
• Jenkins pushes artifacts to artefactory.

2.1.108. Explain critical success factors of DevOps?

• Management commitment to culture change
• Creation of a collaborative, learning culture
• Common values and vocabulary
• Systems engineering that spans Dev and Ops
• Meaningful metrics
• A balance between automation and human interaction
• Application of agile and lean methods
• Open and frequent communication

2.1.109. What is Virtualization? Explain its benefits.

Virtualization
Software is used to mask the physical implementation of an environment (servers, networks, data sources, and so on.) to optimize the use of resources.

Benefits
• Enables more efficient use of physical resources
• More flexibility of deciding when and how to deploy
• Can help provide higher resiliency and scalability
• Enables advanced DevOps practices such as automation, rollbacks, reduced MTTR, and so on

2.1.110. What are Virtualization types?

• Hardware (Server) Virtualization
• Storage Virtualization
• Data Virtualization
• Service Virtualization
• Network Virtualization
• Desktop & User Virtualization
• Application Virtualization.

2.1.111. What is Tivoli Service Automation Manager?

It enables users to request, deploy, monitor, and manage cloud computing services with traceable processes.

2.1.112. What is SoftLayer Portal?

Ability to order and interact with products and services, manage, and maintain SoftLayer account.

https://www.youtube.com/watch?v=gscUrEL3IT8&list=PL6j6__J0kCu_yfau-LShdnZCOhFYh-RZa

2.1.113. What is Technical debt? Why it is important?

Technical debt is the cost of not making improvements to your environment which, over time, results in:

• Learn principles for attaining continuous operations capabilities
• Understand the shared duties between development and operations
• Improve team awareness and proactive involvement in monitoring the codebase, test suite, application, infrastructure, and so on.
• Discover helpful resources to continue learning more about operations for infrastructures implementing DevOps continuous operations, and continuous delivery applications.

2.1.114. Explain types of Operational Technical Debt?

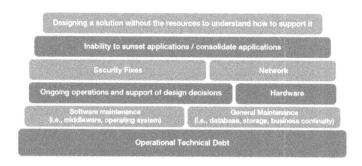

Figure 2.69: Operational Technical Debt Types

2.1.115. What is Gold Plating?

Gold Plating is working on a task beyond the point where the extra effort is worth any value it adds.

2.1.116. What is the cultural challenge for DevOps?

People need to work together across traditional role boundaries. Developers need to work with operations and testing teams.

2.1.117. At which phase would container management tools be required?

Containers are created in the packaging phase.

2.1.118. What is Infrastructure as a Service (IaaS)?

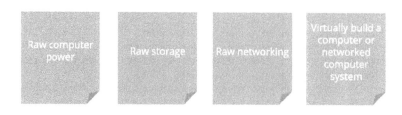

Figure 2.70: IaaS Overview

Payment is for resources provisioned:
- When you use a component, no one else can use it
- Fair to pay for components requested even if unused
- Main difference is that virtual components are easy to return to the Cloud vendor
  - Short term *rental* can be very economic
  - Easy to reconfigure to smaller or larger computers

2.1.119. What is Platform as a Service (PaaS)?

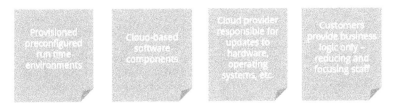

Figure 2.71: PaaS Overview

Payment is for resources used.

2.1.120. What is Software as a Service (SaaS)?

Figure 2.72: SaaS Overview

• Pay for actual usage
  - Message sent/received
  - Storage of information
  - Other factors

2.1.121.   What is an example of IaaS?

IaaS provides raw computing, storage, and networking.

2.1.122.   What is segregation of duty?

Require several entities to complete a sensitive operation.

2.1.123.   What are the differences between Architecture versus design?

Architecture	Design
Strategic design	Tactical design
Global –"how"	Local –"what"
Programming paradigms, architectural patterns	Algorithms, design patterns, programming idioms
Non-functional requirements	Functional requirements
Represented in UML as component, deployment, and package diagrams	Represented in UML as class, object, and behaviour diagrams which appear in detailed functional design documents

2.1.124.   What do you mean by Client Server Architecture?

Client server architecture utilizes a thick client communicating with data storage.

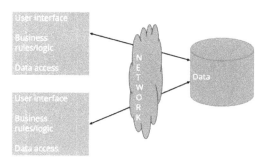

Figure 2.73: Client Server architecture overview

2.1.125.   What are the advantages of Client Server Architecture?

Advantages

- Separation of user interface presentation and business logic processing from the centralized data layer
- Reusability of server components
- Ease of managing security of centrally located data
- Optimize infrastructure usage
- Scalable

2.1.126. What are the disadvantages of Client Server Architecture?

Disadvantages

- Lack of infrastructure for dealing with requirements changes
- Security
- Server availability and reliability as it is a single point of failure
- Testability and scalability
- Presentation and business logic in same place.

2.1.127. What are the advantages of Service Oriented Architecture?

Advantages

- Loose coupling
- Interoperability—business services across platforms
- Location transparency
- Reuse of IT Services—can expose legacy applications
- Development cost reductions
- Speed to market
- Better business and IT integration.

2.1.128. What are the disadvantages of Service Oriented Architecture?

Disadvantages

- Costly to migrate
- Need good control system
- Requires complex service auditing and monitoring
- Additional development and design.

2.1.129. What do you mean by 4+1 Architecture View Model?

The 4+1 architecture view model describes the architecture in terms of four different views:

- Logical view is end user functionality
- Development view is software management
- Process view is system processes and communication
- Physical view or deployment view is software topology on hardware
- The resulting scenarios or use cases form the +1 view.

2.1.130. Define Architecture?

Architecture is infrastructure which interconnects system components. It is often realized as messaging system and associated systems.

2.1.131. What are the features of effective user stories?

• Agile development often specify requirements in terms of user stories
• Effective user stories need to be testable

• Features of effective user stories are as follows:

- It needs to describe an action which has value to a specific user
- It needs to target a specific user or role
- It needs to have clearly stated acceptance criteria which can easily be tested
- It needs to be small enough to implement in a few days
- It needs to be short and precise.

2.1.132. Give examples of Technical Debt user stories?

As an application owner, *I want to* upgrade the DB2 version of my application so that I have the most current product capabilities and avoid outages and performance degradation that there are known fixes or improvements for.

As an application owner, I need an archival process for data over 1 year old so that I can reduce the size of my database by xx%, which will save "x" dollars per month and improve transaction performance by xx%.

As an application owner, I want to apply the "xxx" security patch to my infrastructure so that IBM is not in the news as being hacked and there is not a negative impact on the stock price.

As a support team member for a Domain, I need a consolidated view of log information in the form of a portal so that we improve problem resolution time by xx%.

2.1.133. Define Mean Time To Recover (MTTR)?

The ability to execute successful end-to end business transactions.
After problem identification, how long does it take to:

- Find the root cause
- Recreate the issue in development
- Design / Code and Test Solution
- Deploy fixed component or feature back into Production.

2.1.134. Explain Functional Test Types?

Business goals fulfillment is the main purpose of functional test cases.

Figure 2.74: Functional test types

2.1.135. Explain Non-Functional Test Types?

Performance, resource utilization, usability, compatibility etc. fulfillment is the main purpose of Non--functional test cases.

Figure 2.75: Non Functional test types

2.1.136. Explain Software Testing Principles?

1. Testing shows presence of defects
2. Exhaustive testing is impossible

3. Early testing
4. Defect clustering
5. Pesticide Paradox
6. Testing is context dependent
7. Absence--of--errors fallacy.

2.1.137.　Explain DevOps Testing Pillars?

Figure 2.76: DevOps testing Pillars

2.1.138.　Explain test coverage?

It is a measure of how much of executable code was tested.

2.1.139.　Explain Myths of Test Coverage?

Myth: Test coverage = Quality Target
Reality: Test coverage helps find untested code

Myth: A test suite that passes without any failures is indicative of high quality code **Reality:** Cannot guarantee that all of the code is tested by test suite

Myth: A good measure for test suite quality is code coverage achieved by tests **Reality:** Even with 100% code coverage and all tests passing, there can be undiscovered bug

2.1.140.　Explain Black Box Testing?

Testing method where the internal structure / design is NOT known to the tester.

2.1.141. Explain White Box Testing?

Testing method where the internal structure / design is known to the tester.

2.1.142. What are the differences between Black Box Testing and White Box Testing?

Black Box Testing	White Box Testing
Applicable to higher levels of testing (e.g., acceptance, integration & system).	Applicable to lower levels of testing (e.g., mainly unit, component, some integration & system).
Programming knowledge not Required.	Programming knowledge required.
User stories / specifications used as basis for test cases .	Detail design / code used as basis for test cases (inputs, outputs).
• All-pairs Testing • Orthogonal Array /Combinatorial Testing	• Branch (Decision) • Path • Full Regression • Statement

2.1.143. How do we know when to start testing?

Test begins when the project begins. For example: TDD, BDD

89. How do we know when to stop testing?

- Don't stop testing --Assess production readiness for iteration
- Risk assessment for any deviations from plan/standard process
- Thoroughness measures – code/risk coverage
- Cost & iteration boundary
- Reached an explicit level of testing

2.1.144. Define Modular Testing Framework?

- Independent scripts aligned to module structure of application being tested
- Modules used hierarchically to build larger test cases

2.1.145. Explain advantages of Modular Testing Framework?

- Quick startup
- Enables changes at lowest levels as not to impact other test cases

2.1.146.   Explain disadvantages of Modular Testing Framework?

Data is embedded in the test script, maintenance is difficult.

2.1.147.   Define Data Driven Testing Framework?

- Test input and expected results are stored in a separate file usually in tabular format
- A single script can execute with multiple sets of data
- Driver script navigates through program, reads data input and logs test status

2.1.148.   Explain advantages of Data Driven Testing Framework?

Reduces the number of test scripts required (over Modular).

2.1.149.   Explain disadvantages of Data Driven Testing Framework?

Tight coupling between scripts and data may exist.

2.1.150.   Define Keyword Driven Testing Framework?

- Utilizes data tables and self-explanatory keywords that describe actions
- Test data stored separately just like the Keywords/Actions (Directives)
- Keyword Driven Testing separates test creation process into two distinct stages:
    1. Design & development stage
    2. Execution stage

2.1.151.   Explain advantages of Keyword Driven Testing Framework?

Both data and keywords can be reused across scripts providing flexibility.

2.1.152.   Explain disadvantages of keyword driven Testing Framework?

Increased flexibility can drive complexity.

2.1.153.   Define Hybrid Testing Framework?

- Combination of modular, data driven and keyword driven frameworks.
- Data driven scripts can access information provided by keyword driven approach.

2.1.154. Explain advantages of Hybrid Testing Framework?

Incorporates all testing framework approaches.

2.1.155. Explain disadvantages of Hybrid Testing Framework?

Most complex approach

2.1.156. Explain Penetration (PEN) Test?

Uses ethical hacking techniques to penetrate an application for the purpose of finding security vulnerabilities that a malicious hacker could potentially exploit.

2.1.157. Explain test automation myths?

Myth: Every manual test can/should be automated.
Reality: Consider cost savings and make tradeoff.

Myth: Test automation is just a matter of purchasing the *right* tool.
Reality: Rare that an off the shelf tool will meet all requirements.

Myth: Test automation always leads to cost savings.
Reality: Time to train test teams, documenting test cases, learning test tools are sometimes not considered.

NOTES

NOTES

Chapter 3 - Introduction

What is HANA - SAP HANA (High-Performance Analytical Appliance) is an in-memory database engine from SAP that is used to analyze large data sets in real time that reside entirely in memory. Very crudely it is a Database System which totally changes the DBMS methodology and it can be deployable on premises or over cloud.

What is new in HANA – HANA is the first system to let you to perform real-time online application processing (OLAP) analysis on an online transaction processing (OLTP) data structure. As a result, you can address today's demand for real-time business insights by creating business applications that previously were neither feasible nor cost-effective.

Figure 3.1: SAP S/4HANA Evolution
Ref: SAP S/4HANA 1709 Release Highlights - SAP AG - Run Simple

SAP S/4HANA 1709
Key Innovations

Figure 3.2: SAP S/4HANA Evolution

Ref: SAP S/4HANA 1709 Release Highlights – SAP AG - Run Simple

3.1. SAP S4_HANA Interview questions and answers

3.1.1. How Users can address the common impediments while Applying Agile to ERP projects?

- Assessing Agile Readiness
- Tailor the approach to the Adoption Lifecycle
- Identify the case for change
- Identify a Champion for Agile
- Change in Roles and Responsibilities
- Select the right first project -demonstrate success
- Set realistic expectations of delivery
- Build a GREAT backlog
- Integrate Organizational Change Management.

3.1.2. What are the critical success factors for an Agile SAP team?

- Establish *Buy-In* to the process at all levels

- Establish confidence and proactively start with win-win situation and do something that can deliver a quick win –
- The *Art of Storytelling*
- Do not be discouraged at the moment of *First Awkward Use*
- Integrating members of team that are not co-located
- Ability to remove impediments
- Manage the flow of work
- Establish a process and framework that works best with your culture, resources, and environment
- Continuously update process and framework –Learn and Adjust

3.1.3. Explain valuable key lessons learned while Applying Agile to ERP projects?

a. Be proactive in creating a model which works for the organizational culture
b. Varying steps of adoption needs to be considered
c. Find the Agile Champion
d. Be proactive in selecting the right first project, not all projects are good candidates for Agile
e. Train the team at all levels
f. Develop a willing to work Product Council
g. Find the right Product Owner
h. Give more focus on team work rather than mechanics
i. Collaboration over co-location
j. Build effectively the Backlog – Story Mapping and Stories
k. Set rules to make productive optimum team engagement
l. Selecting the proper metrics and the proper reporting tools
m. Process validated Lean Agile processes are incremental, iterative and adaptive
- Team was not disrupted by the scope changes
- Team generally made change adoption in just 3-4 sprints

n. Key Project / Program stakeholders
- Confirm empirical evidence is better that Progress Reports
- Give proper slack time to teams and allow proper time in Scrum planning events to focus on "Value Add" work
- Team becomes "Being Agile" mindset and "Lean Thinkers" rather than just "doing Agile"
- Work products completed significantly ahead of stipulated Project milestone time.

3.1.4. Explain the purpose of SCRUM of SCRUMs?

Scrum of Scrums focuses on integration topics and cohesive solution build. It consists of the lead consultants and product owners from the individual scrum teams.

3.1.5. Name the currently available SAP S/4HANA deployment options?

SAP currently plans to offer on-premise, cloud (public and managed), and hybrid deployments.

3.1.6. Name some SAP S/4HANA goals?

HANA Goals
- Enables New Application and Optimize Existing Application
- High Performance and Scalability
- Hybrid Data Management System
- Compatible with Standard DBMS feature
- Support for Text analysis, indexing and search
- Cloud support and application isolation
    - Executing application logic inside the data layer.

3.1.7. Is your move to SAP S/4HANA driven by the Business or by IT?

It's virtually impossible to start a business transformation out of an IT project. IT-sponsored projects are typically system conversions that lay the foundation for later innovation projects driven by the business.

3.1.8. Can you convert from the SAP ERP application to SAP S/4HANA in a single step?

Technically, single-step conversion is possible for SAP ERP 6.0 (any enhancement pack) single-stack, Unicode systems; database and OS-level restrictions may apply. Systems that don't fulfill these criteria have likely experienced little maintenance in the past years. In practice, systems with dated software release levels may require somewhat more effort than the ones recently updated.
If the system can't be converted technically in a single step, a new implementation is a better choice, because the combined cost of an upgrade to SAP ERP 6.0 or a Unicode upgrade followed by a conversion to SAP S/4HANA would be prohibitively high. Moreover, combining two upgrades in a single downtime will most probably exceed the maximum system outage your business can afford.
The second factor to consider here is your rollout strategy. If you plan to roll out the system on a company-code-by-company-code basis, then a new implementation approach is a better option. However, if this rollout strategy is a precaution rather than a hard constraint, you should take into account the implied cost of integrating the old and new system landscape, such as for intercompany scenarios, master data synchronization, and consolidation. Often, putting more attention on testing is a far more effective risk mitigation strategy.

3.1.9. Do you require previous transactional data in the new system?

When choosing between conversion and new implementation, the requirement to retain all data in the system is a very strong indication for a system conversion. The first response is often, "Yes, we do need all data in the new system." However, you should challenge this standpoint and design a data strategy that takes into account the available technological alternatives.

3.1.10. Are landscape consolidation and process harmonization key value drivers?

For companies with a track record of mergers and acquisitions, it's often easier for different divisions to agree on a new neutral set of best practices than to debate which of the current ERPs should become the consolidation target. In this case, opt for a new implementation and consolidate the system configurations and data required to start business operations into this new SAP S/4HANA system.

3.1.11. Do you have a high or low number of Interfaces to other Systems (SAP and Third-Party)?

In new implementations, interfaces have to be (re)developed and tested, especially interfaces to third-party solutions. With a system conversion, adjusting existing interfaces typically takes less effort.
Thus, a high number of interfaces in the current system makes a stronger case for conversion. However, before settling on this decision, consider the new integration technologies SAP offers, especially the SAP Cloud Platform Integration and SAP Cloud Platform Integration Advisor services.

3.1.12. Can your company sustain a multiyear Innovation plan with incremental innovations?

Although this aspect is entirely nontechnical, it may in the end overturn all of the above considerations. If incremental innovation is part of your company's philosophy, a system conversion followed by innovative projects will lead to the desired outcome. However, other companies may not deem themselves capable of persistently executing a multiyear plan because they expect a shift in focus or a major change in strategy. In such cases, a new implementation is the only chance to harvest the full value of SAP S/4HANA.

3.1.13. Give an example of ERP landscape consolidation?

<u>Example 1: ERP Landscape consolidation</u>

One common situation is a consolidation of multiple SAP ERP systems into one. A standard transition path is either:

• Implementing the new system based on best practices followed by loading master data and open items from all source systems
• Converting one of the systems and loading open items from the others

If your requirement is to load historic data from all SAP ERP systems that are subject to consolidation, you will have to resort to a selective data transition and employ specialized tools and services.

3.1.14. Does SAP S/4HANA Cloud support all industries types?

Yes.

3.1.15. Does SAP "SAP S/4HANA managed by SAP HANA Enterprise Cloud" support all industries types?

Yes.

3.1.16. What is the frequency of software updates of SAP S/4HANA Cloud?

Quarterly, fixed schedule.

3.1.17. What is the frequency of software updates of SAP S/4HANA Cloud, single tenant edition?

Twice a year, one mandatory.
Must update within the next 6 months.

3.1.18. What is the frequency of software updates of SAP S/4HANA managed by SAP HANA enterprise Cloud?

Recommended once in a year.

3.1.19. What is the Licensing type of SAP S/4HANA Cloud?

Software as a service (SaaS) (subscription).

3.1.20. What is the Licensing type of SAP S/4HANA Cloud, single tenant edition?
SaaS (subscription).

3.1.21. What is the Licensing type of SAP S/4HANA managed by SAP HANA enterprise cloud?
Bring your own license (BYOL) and infrastructure as a service (IaaS) (subscription).

3.1.22. What are the Implementation options of SAP S/4HANA Cloud?

New implementation with data migration.

3.1.23. What are the Implementation options of SAP S/4HANA Cloud, single tenant edition?

New implementation with data migration.

3.1.24. What are the Implementation options of SAP S/4HANA managed by SAP HANA enterprise cloud?

New implementation with data migration, system conversion, or move of a current SAP S/4HANA system.

3.1.25. What are the best practices followed for any new implementations and conversion projects?

• Build up your team's skills. This will pay off economically and in many other ways.
• Ensure architectural due diligence. Review the five key topics in the "Architectural Due Diligence" section below that your architecture team can't afford to neglect.
• Understand, explore, and leverage SAP Model Company services in both new implementations and conversions.
• Redesign your business processes for in- memory computing. This is about rethinking, not about doing the same things faster.
• Make sure that your development team fully understands the new software development concepts and technologies.
• Recognize that SAP Fiori is more than a new Web UI. Establish an adoption strategy for SAP Fiori and appoint a UX architect to carry it out.
• Curate your master data prior to the transition to SAP S/4HANA.
• Make sure that there is enough focus on pertinent hardware planning and performance testing.

3.1.26. What are the best practices followed for any conversion projects?

• Take care of your financial data and understand the plans of your finance team to leverage the new G/L, parallel accounting, and document split capabilities.
• Realize that conversion test cycles are the backbone of your project. Follow the guidelines to establish a successful project plan.
• Check the compatibility of your add-ons in advance and decide how to deal with each add-on before the conversion.
• Scrutinize your simplification items and pay close attention to the ones that require a business decision or a preparation project.
• Take advantage of the opportunity to reassess and clean up your custom code. Decide what you need and delete the rest.

3.1.27. What are the two deployment options customers can choose?

a. Deploy a sandbox system using the SAP Cloud Appliance Library tool. This option requires a third-party infrastructure as a service (IaaS), such as Amazon Web Services, Microsoft Azure, or Google

Cloud. SAP Cloud Appliance Library completely automates the provisioning of the virtual machines and deployment of the corresponding system image.

b. Download and install the selected SAP Model Company on premise.

A 30-day trial of SAP Model Company is available on SAP Store.

SAP Model Company is not only essential for new installations, but very helpful for conversions too. Use SAP Model Company during the project's preparation and exploration phase to:

• Demonstrate the functionality and process in show-and-tell sessions for business users
• Have your key users study the preconfigured scenarios with the test scripts
• Build prototypes by using or extending the existing configuration
• Use it as a reference when conducting fit-gap/ fit-to-standard analysis.

3.1.28. How you can utilize "Integrate" option of SAP Cloud Platform for your SAP S/4HANA project?

<u>Integrate</u>
To enable SAP S/4HANA integration:

• Use SAP Cloud Platform Integration as the integration layer for on-premise-to-cloud and cloud-to-cloud integration.
• Use standard prepackaged integration content for SAP and third-party system integration. SAP Cloud Platform Integration provides more than 1,100 integration scenarios including government, business-to-business (B2B), and non-SAP-software integration.
• Use the SAP Cloud Platform Open Connectors service for tight integration into more than 160 non-SAP cloud applications.

3.1.29. How you can utilize "Extend" option of SAP Cloud Platform for your SAP S/4HANA project?

<u>Extend</u>

To create extensions:

• Use SAP Cloud Platform to keep your core clean and to reinforce the "clean core" policy. Use white-listed APIs and avoid native access to non-public APIs. This will pay off in future upgrades.
• Check SAP Store for SAP solutions and SAP App Center or Certified Solutions Directory for available partner solutions.
• Use SAP Cloud Platform, ABAP environment, to leverage the ABAP skills of your development team.
• Rely on the wider developer community to build Java or node.js applications and extensions. Make sure you use the SAP S/4HANA Cloud software development kit (SDK) and SAP Cloud Platform API Management service.

• Utilize SAP Cloud Platform as a central platform for extending all SAP products (whether SAP S/4HANA, SAP SuccessFactors solutions, or any other).

3.1.30. How you can utilize "Innovate" option of SAP Cloud Platform for your SAP S/4HANA project?

<u>Innovate</u>

To support innovation:
• Use SAP Cloud Platform to create minimum viable products and proof-of-concept apps for your business quickly. Connecting these "playground" accounts to the systems with test data will help convince the business more than anything else.
• Combine the platform's mobile services and SAP Leonardo Services with third-party data and services from our partner ecosystem to create new apps quickly.

3.1.31. How you can leverage the strength of the SAP Ecosystem for your SAP S/4HANA project?

SAP has a powerful partner ecosystem ready to help enterprises of any size to make the move to SAP S/4HANA.

The largest 17 SAP partners specializing in system integration – also referred to as global strategic service partners (GSSPs) – have more than 60,000 trained SAP S/4HANA professionals globally, with more than 5,000 SAP S/4HANA consultants certified by SAP. All of them offer unique value-adding solutions, tools, and accelerators to speed up transition from SAP ERP to SAP S/4HANA.

These 17 partners include Accenture, Atos, Capgemini, Cognizant, Deloitte, DXC Technology, EY, HCL Technologies, IBM, Infosys, LTI, NTT Data, PwC, Tata Consultancy Services (TCS), Tech Mahindra, T-Systems, and Wipro.

In addition, there are hundreds of regional system integration partners who offer specialized expertise and services to make the transition to SAP S/4HANA easier for our SAP ERP customers in all segments of the market. Notable regional system integration partners include Abeam Consulting, BearingPoint, Birlasoft, Bristlecone, Fujitsu, Hitachi, MHP, and Neoris.

SAP's wider ecosystem includes more than 2,000 members of the SAP PartnerEdge program who specialize in selling and servicing SAP S/4HANA mainly to small and medium-size enterprises. These partners have made significant investments in SAP S/4HANA practices too, such as educating their consultants in the "10 Steps to SAP S/4HANA" program offered by SAP.

3.1.32. What is SAP TRANSFORMATION NAVIGATOR tool?

SAP Transformation Navigator is a Web-based and free self-service road-mapping tool. It uses the information about your SAP system landscape that is stored in your instance of SAP Solution Manager to create a recommendation for a new SAP S/4HANA-centric landscape with the latest SAP solutions. It also provides information about possible benefits that you can achieve with the new solution capabilities. At the end of your analysis, you can download a comprehensive report that contains recommendations for SAP products that are tailored to your system requirements.

3.1.33. What is NEXTGEN business scenario recommendations tool for SAP S/4HANA?

The business scenario recommendations for SAP S/4HANA report has been redesigned to help you discover where SAP S/4HANA can make a difference in your company.
It analyses the functional system usage of your SAP ERP application and computes the key process performance indicators (PPIs) for the relevant process areas, such as degree of automation, process failures, and on-time execution. Next, it highlights the new or improved functionality of
SAP S/4HANA, SAP Leonardo technologies, and other SAP innovations that can help improve the performance and efficiency of the respective business processes. You can download your report as a PDF for offline viewing.
Thus, the tool allows for a very focused discussion between business decision-makers and IT based on hard facts and measurable business objectives.

3.1.34. What is SAP Readiness Check tool for SAP S/4HANA?

The SAP Readiness Check tool for SAP S/4HANA performs functional and technical assessments for SAP ERP systems prior to a planned conversion to SAP S/4HANA.

The tool's main focus is on the functional assessment that evaluates all available SAP S/4HANA simplification items and identifies the ones that are relevant for your system. This assessment provides a basis for the functional system redesign that is necessary upon conversion.

The technical assessment includes system sizing and data volume management, assertion of the software prerequisites for conversion, inspection of SAP Business Warehouse (BW) extractors, and a first-pass estimate of the impact on the custom code.

The software prerequisites cover OS and database versions of the ERP system, as well as the installed industry solutions, add-ons, and activated business functions. The list of non-supported SAP industry solutions and business functions is reduced continually, and there are only very few left with SAP S/4HANA 1809.

The technology used by "SAP Readiness Check" to estimate the impact on custom code (SYCM report) is a trade-off between the speed and precision of the code scan. The results of the report are sufficient to get a first impression of the magnitude of the necessary changes. For an exact analysis and subsequent adaptation of custom code, SAP recommends the ABAP test cockpit.

Even if you decide on a new implementation, SAP recommends running SAP Readiness Check for your SAP ERP. The results will help you better understand the state of your current system from an SAP S/4HANA point of view. In particular, the check highlights the incompatible addons and functionality that you need to replace.

3.1.35. What are the different options for system conversion SAP offers in order to help users meet system downtime requirements?

To help you meet system downtime requirements, SAP offers the following options for system conversion:

• Standard conversion for smaller SAP ERP systems
• Downtime-optimized conversion for midsize and large systems
• Minimized downtime service by SAP Digital Business Services for extra-large systems.

As a rule of thumb, a small system has data volumes of less than 5 TB, and extra-large systems have data volumes of more than 20 TB.

3.1.36. What is Software update Manager?

Software Update Manager is a multipurpose tool used for SAP software maintenance (for example, for installing support packages, migrating an SAP system to another database, installing add-ons, and other tasks). It is also the tool that technically converts an SAP ERP system into an SAP S/4HANA system. It combines the migration of the system to the SAP HANA database (if required), conversion of data, and software upgrade into one single step.

A single-step conversion is supported for SAP ERP 6.x (any enhancement pack) single-stack, Unicode systems; however, database and OS-level restrictions may apply.
Most of the data conversion (that is, the transfer into the new data model) is carried out by Software Update Manager with the help of special programs, namely XPRAs and XCLAs. The conversion is partially executed directly in SAP HANA and partially in the ABAP application server(s). However, both the conversion of financial data and the conversion of material ledger data are special steps that are performed after the actual conversion procedure of Software Update Manager.

Downtime-Optimized Conversion with Software Update Manager For larger systems, converting the data into the new data structures may take a long runtime.

In practice, project teams and business users can usually negotiate a cutover window between 8 hours (that is, one factory shift) and 60 hours (that is, from Friday 6 p.m. to Monday 6 a.m.). This time window includes not only the actual downtime but all phases of the cutover procedure.

To make this cutover window achievable for midsize and large systems, SAP has developed the downtime-optimized conversion option and has included it in the standard Software Update Manager tool.9 In a nutshell, it converts large parts of the SAP ERP data during uptime and uses record-and-reply technology to incorporate the data changes. This way, midsize and large systems are able to comply with the common downtime requirements using the standard tool set.

3.1.37. What is Minimized downtime service by SAP Digital Business Services?

The minimized downtime service offered by SAP Digital Business Services is designed to help customers operating extra-large systems with:

• Data volumes of 20 TB or more
• A large data footprint in finance and/or logistics
• A high volume of application changes.

The minimized downtime service also makes it possible to combine multiple maintenance events – such as Unicode conversion, a move to another data center, and system conversion – into a single system downtime.

The technology applied within this service is known as near-zero downtime technology (NZDT). In essence, this conversion procedure is composed of the following steps:

• Activating change recording in the productive SAP ERP system with database triggers
• Creating a copy (clone) of the production system
• Performing a standard system conversion with Software Update Manager using the clone as the source system
• Synchronizing the newly converted system with the original production system
• Performing the cutover to the newly converted system
With this approach, a cutover window of 24 hours is usually achievable. However, given the complexity of the procedure, the exact runtimes have to be confirmed individually for any given environment.

3.1.38. What is ABAP Test Cockpit tool?

The ABAP test cockpit (ATC) offers SAP S/4HANA- specific checks available with SAP NetWeaver 7.51 or higher. While you can use these checks with a stand-alone installation of SAP NetWeaver 7.51 or 7.52, ATC in SAP S/4HANA brings important additional features. SAP recommends running ATC out of the sandbox once it has been converted to SAP S/4HANA.

With SAP S/4HANA, the ABAP development tools in Eclipse enable automated adaptation of custom code with only a few clicks through the ABAP quick fixes. These can resolve the most frequent findings that don't necessarily require deep functional knowledge, such as ORDER_BY issues, MATNR issues, and issues related to data model changes, such as database access to tables KONV, VBFA, VBUK, VBUP, BSEG, and others. SAP's goal is to achieve an automation rate of 60% to 80% in any given system.

The new "Custom Code Migration" app built with SAP Fiori offers analytical capabilities that can help you understand the impact on the custom code and structure your work accordingly. The app also helps you remove unused custom code upon system conversion. To do this, it can load the code execution statistics directly from the SAP ERP production system and delete the custom code that has not been executed in the monitored period of time during the conversion. To benefit from this feature, SAP advises you to activate the ABAP call monitor in the productive SAP ERP system today and thus start collecting these statistics as soon as possible.

Note that the above features are part of SAP S/4HANA and do not require a separate license.

3.1.39. What is SQL Monitor tool?

The ABAP test cockpit also offers performance checks to identify poorly performing ABAP code. However, optimizing the entire body of custom code is usually impractical because of the associated effort. Instead, you can achieve considerable performance improvements with only a fraction of the effort by using SQL Monitor, which analyses all database queries in the production system.

The SQL Performance Tuning Worklist highlights the most critical ABAP statements by combining the results of the static code checks with the runtime SQL performance data supplied by SQL Monitor.

3.1.40. What is SAP S/4HANA Migration Cockpit tool?

For SAP S/4HANA data migrations, SAP recommends using the SAP S/4HANA migration cockpit. It comes as part of both SAP S/4HANA and SAP S/4HANA Cloud without any extra license and cost. This is also the only tool to migrate data to SAP S/4HANA Cloud.

The tool allows migrating data from both SAP and third-party systems and offers step-by-step guidance throughout the data migration process. That includes automatic generation of migration programs, simulation mode for migration to verify data quality and help ensure error-free data loading, cross-object value mappings to optimize data consistency, progress monitoring, and more.
The tool enables you to choose between two scenarios for data upload: files or staging tables. A third option – direct transfer of data from SAP source systems – is currently available for piloting within SAP's customer care program.
It supports migrating to SAP S/4HANA (on premise) as well as to SAP S/4HANA Cloud.

The software comes with a ready-made set of migration objects and rules. A migration object represents a business entity in SAP S/4HANA, such as a customer, sales order, or invoice. It encapsulates the logic to create the specific business entities through the corresponding APIs offered by SAP S/4HANA. All migration objects are ready for immediate use. The tool allows you to extend existing migration objects and rules and to create custom-specific objects with the migration object modeler (the latter is available for SAP S/4HANA on premise only).
Working with the SAP S/4HANA migration cockpit is easy and does not require developer skills. These are only needed when you want to create your own migration objects or transformation rules.
With the above functions and features, SAP S/4HANA migration cockpit has generally superseded SAP's legacy system migration workbench. The usage of the latter with SAP S/4HANA is neither supported nor recommended by SAP.

3.1.41. What is SAP Data Services?

Customers migrating from multiple legacy systems by different third-party vendors to their SAP S/4HANA instance will face an increased level of complexity in data migration. The goal of data migration should not just be to move and transform the data, but also to improve data quality so that you go live with clean, valid, trusted data. SAP's flagship ETL solution for profiling, extracting, transforming, and improving data quality is SAP Data Services. This solution can play an important role in a data migration project.

Employing SAP Data Services in your migration project gives you the ability to:

• Profile the source system data to discover data quality problems within those systems – from simple technical profiling (such as how many records miss a certain attribute) to complex cross-table checks (such as how many vendors have no corresponding orders)
• Extract source system data efficiently and transform it into the target SAP S/4HANA format and structure
• Apply data cleansing jobs
• Implement data validations against the target system configuration to help ensure technical alignment of the transformation logic
• Deliver the data in the correct format (staging tables or files) to the SAP S/4HANA migration cockpit to reduce the amount of work needed to be done there.

As data migration projects become larger, collaboration is required in designing, transforming, and validating the data. For these projects, it is recommended to use SAP Advanced Data Migration by Syniti.

3.1.42. What is SAP Advanced Data Migration by Syniti?

Midsize and large projects require extensive collaboration within the data team and with other stakeholders. A combination of the SAP Advanced Data Migration application by Syniti with SAP Data Services provides the orchestration, extraction, trans formation, and data quality capabilities that are essential for migrating complex data to SAP S/4HANA.

SAP Advanced Data Migration is built specifically to automate a best-practice process for data migration and to orchestrate the process of SAP and third-party data migrations to SAP S/4HANA. It offers a collaboration platform enabling all stakeholders to deliver their tasks in a guided, controlled, auditable, and secure environment.

The key features of the solution are:
• A single view into what your team is working on: mappings, data cleansing, data construction, sign-off workflows, and more. The solution provides the metrics and KPIs you need to drive project progress.
• The solution automates the creation of up to 80% of the code and reports needed to execute data migration.

• The ready-to-load data is handed over to the SAP S/4HANA migration cockpit either through files or staging tables.
• Technical reconciliation capabilities support the comparison and review of source and target data, as well as the approval of the migration process by the business owners.
• You can reuse the business knowledge and assets created during the migration for both subsequent migrations and future information management initiatives (that is, post-go-live data quality initiatives).

Projects employing the solution indicate savings of 30% to 40% versus traditional approaches.

3.1.43. What are the key benefits of SAP advanced data migration by Syniti to Project Manager?

• Automated reporting into the exact status of your migration program
• Timelines and data quality metrics

3.1.44. What are the key benefits of SAP advanced data migration by Syniti to business user/ subject matter expert?

• No more spreadsheets to populate and manage
• Web portal to design, view, check, and remediate data – with a minimum effort.

3.1.45. What are the key benefits of SAP advanced data migration by Syniti to developer?

• Auto-generated code for data extraction, transformation, validation, and reconciliation
• Focus on high-value business validation rules

3.1.46. What is SAP Solution Manager?

SAP Solution Manager has been designed to support the entire lifecycle of SAP solutions and is available to every customer with an SAP maintenance contract.

SAP Solution Manager offers a number of tools to support individual project tasks, such as business process documentation, test management, and software deployment. As of version 7.2, it also offers the Focused Build solution, which enables a preconfigured requirement-to-deploy process within SAP Solution Manager. It includes business demand and requirements management, integrated risk management, and collaboration features that help business and IT work together more closely while also helping manage global development teams. This methodology and approach were ideated in "SAP MaxAttention" engagements and cater to the needs of SAP S/4HANA projects with a high innovation ratio.

3.1.47. What are the parameters you need to consider for focused build using SAP Solution Manager?

Consider Focused Build for SAP Solution Manager if any of the points below holds true:

• You consider the project a business-driven project.
• You plan your new implementation based on the best practices of SAP Model Company or SAP Activate, and the content is provided through SAP Solution Manager.
• You expect a considerable number (more than 100) of RICEFWs to be developed.
• The project team works across several locations, or you expect a high share of remote delivery.
• The project management office wants to use a project tool that supports standardized and transparent activities in the project and helps accelerate onboarding.
• You already employ, or intend to employ, SAP Solution Manager for IT operations after the go-live.
• You intend to apply agile development principles in your project.

Using a tool with guided project procedures decreases the risk of deployment failures, enables a real-time status view of all project activities, and helps to keep a centralized source of truth for business processes and documentations.

3.1.48. What is the use of "Managing historical data" in SAP S/4HANA Cloud 1902?

Data aging offers the option of moving large amounts of data within a database to gain more working memory. With this, you can manage current and historical data using the data aging framework.

3.1.49. What is the use of "Output Channels" in SAP S/4HANA Cloud 1902?

● Printer - cloud-enabled using print queues/cloud printing manager
● Email - allows flexible configuration of sender and recipients
● EDI - Electronic Data Interchange.

3.1.50. What is the use of "Output Parameter Determination" in SAP S/4HANA Cloud 1902?

- Allows sending multiple messages to multiple recipients using multiple channels at the same time.
- Flexible definition of business rules without the need for implementation.
- Easily extensible with SAP standard fields and customer fields.

3.1.51. What is the use of "Business Event Handling" in SAP S/4HANA Cloud 1902?

Business event handling enables applications, interested parties, and clients to consume events related to all S/4HANA business objects.

In addition, you can view and manage subscriptions, read outbound queues, and view business events.

3.1.52. What is the use of "Enterprise Event Enablement" in SAP S/4HANA Cloud 1902?

The enterprise event enablement framework enables the exchange of events across different platforms for seamless event-driven communication.

3.1.53. What is the use of "Situation Handling" in SAP S/4HANA Cloud 1902?

Situation handling brings urgent issues to the attention of specific groups of users who are then able to react immediately to the notifications they receive. This not only speeds up the handling of specific situations in your company, but also supports the optimization of your business processes.

3.1.54. What is the use of "License Compliance Digital Access" in SAP S/4HANA Cloud 1902?

With the introduction of a new license model for SAP S/4HANA Cloud, customers can subscribe to the SAP S/ 4HANA Cloud Digital Access Enablement Package for documents. This enables the creation of unique records in Cloud Services by non-SAP technologies (including bots, IoT devices and sensors, intelligent devices, third-party systems, and apps developed by customers or partners). To provide transparency of the actual usage, the License Compliance app for Digital Access shows the number of documents that have been created in the current license period.

3.1.55. What is the use of "Extensibility Cockpit" in SAP S/4HANA Cloud 1902?

You can view extensible objects that correspond with business contexts that are mapped with or without scope items.

3.1.56. What is the use of "CDS View-Based Replication" in SAP S/4HANA Cloud 1902?

With CDS View-Based Replication for SAP S/4HANA Cloud, users can replicate data from an SAP S/4HANA Cloud (source) to the SAP Cloud Platform HANA system (target) based on released CDS views.

3.1.57. What is the use of " Enterprise Search" in SAP S/4HANA Cloud 1902?

Enterprise Search is a search solution that provides unified, comprehensive, and secure real-time access to enterprise data which enables users to search for structured data (business objects) and allows direct access to the associated applications and actions.

3.1.58. What is the use of "Analytical Tools" in SAP S/4HANA Cloud 1902?

The Analytics framework allows the customers to consolidate business data from different virtual data models, work with real-time data, and build reports. With these reports, customers can easily visualize and interpret the data which in turn will help the decision-makers for better analysis.

3.1.59. What is the use of "Query Design" in SAP S/4HANA Cloud 1902?

Query Design enables you to manage the creation of analytical queries and make the results available through tiles on the SAP Fiori Launchpad.

3.1.60. What is the use of "Analysis Path Framework" in SAP S/4HANA Cloud 1902?

Analysis Path Framework provides business users and managers an intuitive, easy to use analytical tool to perform interactive data explorations and drill-down analyses for root cause investigations.

3.1.61. What is the use of "Predictive Analytics integrator (PAi)" in SAP S/4HANA Cloud 1902?

Predictive Analytics integrator (PAi) integrates predictive capabilities into business processes. PAi uses algorithms to predict an unknown outcome, for example, using a predictive model you can forecast when a buyer is likely to negotiate a new procurement contract. Business cases requiring a predictive measure are described as predictive scenarios, which manage the lifecycle of the predictive models included within them.

3.1.62. What is the use of "Plant Maintenance" in SAP S/4HANA Cloud 1902?

Plant Maintenance enables you to plan and perform the maintenance of operational systems, such as machines or production installations. It comprises the inspection, maintenance, and repair measures that need to be taken to keep your assets in working order. These activities are typically performed by maintenance planners and maintenance workers.

3.1.63. What is the use of "Overhead Cost Accounting" in SAP S/4HANA Cloud 1902?

This application area covers the journal entries for Overhead Cost Accounting. It captures costs by cost centre and defines the output of the cost centre in terms of activity types. It allows you to enter statistical key figures as a basis for your allocations at period close.

3.1.64. What is the use of "Profitability and Cost Analysis" in SAP S/4HANA Cloud 1902?

This application area enables you to analyse the profitability of your market segments and single cost objects. It shows contribution margins in real time and offers detailed views for further analysis. You can analyse market segments by product, product group, customer, customer group, and sales organization.

3.1.65. What is the use of "Budget Availability Control" in SAP S/4HANA Cloud 1902?

You can control the budgets in your projects and in your work breakdown structure (WBS) elements. When you post an expense, the available budget is checked. When the budget consumption reaches a defined limit, either a warning or an error message appears.

3.1.66. What is the use of "Asset Accounting" in SAP S/4HANA Cloud 1902?

You can use "Asset Accounting" to manage and monitor tangible fixed assets. It provides detailed information about the transactions relating to tangible fixed assets.

3.1.67. What is the use of "General Ledger Accounting" in SAP S/4HANA Cloud 1902?

You can use "General Ledger Accounting" to perform external accounting tasks.

3.1.68. What is the use of "Inventory Accounting" in SAP S/4HANA Cloud 1902?

You can use "Inventory Accounting" to value and monitor your material and work-in-process inventories according to legal regulations and management accounting requirements. All goods movements are valued in the Material Ledger which supports parallel, real-time valuation of inventories in multiple currencies. A special focus lies on high throughput of logistics data that allows for managing mass data volumes.

You can choose to value your material inventories at standard cost or moving average automatically. In addition, you may make manual adjustments to material costs and inventory values. You may also use periodic valuation of material inventories according to statutory requirements such as Lowest Value or FIFO, or product cost management requirements such as standard costing.

3.1.69. What is the use of "Revenue and Cost Accounting" in SAP S/4HANA Cloud 1902?

You can use "Revenue and Cost Accounting" to recognize revenues and calculate contract liabilities and contract assets.

3.1.70. What is the use of "Cash and Liquidity Management" in SAP S/4HANA Cloud 1902?

To preside over the cash assets of a company, cash managers need to closely monitor cash positions and centrally manage banks and bank accounts for the organization.

3.1.71. What is the use of "Accounts Receivable Accounting" in SAP S/4HANA Cloud 1902?

You can use accounts receivable accounting to process open customer invoices and monitor incoming payments.

3.1.72. What is the use of "Credit Management" in SAP S/4HANA Cloud 1902?

The creditworthiness and payment behaviour of your business partners affect the business results of your company immediately.

3.1.73. What is the use of "Accounts Payable Accounting" in SAP S/4HANA Cloud 1902?

Invoices are created in purchasing and submitted to accounts payable. As an accounts payable accountant, when you receive an invoice, you can view key performance indicators (KPIs) for the invoice and process the invoice.

3.1.74. What is the use of "Discount Collaboration (Business Network Integration)" in SAP S/4HANA Cloud 1902?

SAP S/4HANA Cloud supports the integration with business networks or external systems (currently the Ariba Network) to enable you to collaborate on discount management with your suppliers. You can do this by exchanging invoice-related messages between SAP S/4HANA Cloud and the business network. If the business network or external system (for example, Ariba Network) is integrated and supports the features listed below, SAP S/4HANA Cloud enables you to manage cash discounts from initial offer through to agreement. This optimization of cash discounts can increase your company's profits, and gives your suppliers the opportunity to receive their payments earlier.

3.1.75. What is the use of "Payment Advice Collaboration (Business Network Integration)" in SAP S/4HANA Cloud 1902?

SAP S/4HANA Cloud supports the integration with business networks or external systems (currently the Ariba Network) to enable you to collaborate on payment advices with your suppliers. You can do this by exchanging messages between SAP S/4HANA Cloud and the business network or external system.

If the business network or external system (for example, the Ariba Network) is integrated and supports the features listed below, SAP S/4HANA Cloud enables you to collaborate with your suppliers by sending them payment advices via the business network or external system.

3.1.76. What is the use of "Electronic Bill Presentment and Payment" in SAP S/4HANA Cloud 1902?

Electronic bill presentment and payment enables presenting bills on the Web, thus allowing your customers to pay their bills online.

3.1.77. What is the use of "Settlement Management" in SAP S/4HANA Cloud 1902?

Settlement management provides the sales rebate processing, purchasing rebate processing and sales commission settlement including core business functions that are fully integrated in the order-to-cash cycle. Rebate processing and commission settlement is used to settle subsequent rebates and commissions based on business volume or quantity. Settlement can take place at document item level. Due to the high volume of documents involved, settlement is usually based on cumulative key figures, like business volume, derived from transactional data in documents.

3.1.78. What is the use of "International Trade Classification" in SAP S/4HANA Cloud 1902?

● Classification of products with commodity codes, Intrastat service codes and Customs Tariff Numbers
● Classification of products with control classes and control groupings for legal control
● Management of classification data from external data providers (commodity codes, customs tariff numbers and control classes).

3.1.79. What is the use of "International Trade Compliance" in SAP S/4HANA Cloud 1902?

● Control of statutory regulations for export
● Managing of licenses in accordance with legal control for export (sales orders and deliveries) and import (purchase orders)
● Managing and release of blocked legal control documents
● Managing countries under embargo situations.

3.1.80. What is the use of "International Trade Classification" in SAP S/4HANA Cloud 1902?

You can use classification to manage commodity codes, Intrastat service codes, control classes, control groupings and their assignment to products. The Intrastat service codes are only relevant for Italy.

3.1.81. What is the use of "International Trade Compliance" in SAP S/4HANA Cloud 1902?

You use International Trade Compliance to manage licenses and trade compliance documents. Trade compliance checks are based on the following document types:
● Sales Order
● Outbound Delivery
● Purchase Order.

3.1.82. What is the use of "Intrastat" in SAP S/4HANA Cloud 1902?

You can use Intrastat declarations to record goods movements that cross-national borders between member states of the European Union. In Italy, services must be declared in addition.

You can create Intrastat declarations for the following countries:
● AT (Austria)
● BE (Belgium)
● DE (Germany)
● DK (Denmark)
● ES (Spain)
● FI (Finland)
● FR (France)
● GB (United Kingdom)
● HU (Hungary)
● IE (Ireland)
● IT (Italy)
● LU (Luxembourg)
● NL (The Netherlands)
● PL (Poland)
● RO (Romania)
● SE (Sweden).

3.1.83. What is the purpose of "Integration with SAP Global Trade Services" in SAP S/4HANA Cloud 1902?

Through integration with SAP Global Trade Services, you can transfer master and transaction data from the S/ 4HANA Cloud to your SAP GTS system.

3.1.84. What is the purpose of "Integration with SAP Watch List Screening" in SAP S/4HANA Cloud 1902?

SAP S/4HANA Cloud supports the integration with SAP Watch List Screening (needs to be licensed separately). With the integration, you can screen names and addresses for the following document types:

- Sales orders
- Outbound deliveries
- Purchase orders.

3.1.85. What is the purpose of "Integration with Concur Solutions" in SAP S/4HANA Cloud 1902?

This scenario enables you to connect your SAP S/4HANA Cloud system with your Concur solutions. The integration simplifies expense processes with regard to cost object export as well as financial posting of expense reports and cash advances.

3.1.86. What is the purpose of "Time Sheet" in SAP S/4HANA Cloud 1902?

Use Time Sheet to do activity-based time recording for billing and invoicing of projects assigned to you. You can also record time for non-project tasks, such as administration, training, travel time, and so on.

3.1.87. What is the purpose of "Integration with External HR System" in SAP S/4HANA Cloud 1902?

SAP S/4HANA Cloud supports the integration with an external HR system (currently SAP SuccessFactors Employee Central) to enable you to replicate employee, organizational, and cost centre data.

3.1.88. What is the purpose of "Production BOM Management" in SAP S/4HANA Cloud 1902?

During the product engineering phase, you design and develop products. You design new products or product lines to take advantage of current process technology and to improve quality and reliability. Or, you have to change an existing product due to changing market or customer requirements. The result of this product phase is drawings and a list of all the parts required to produce the product. This list is the bill of material.

3.1.89. What is the purpose of "Material Requirements Planning" in SAP S/4HANA Cloud 1902?

This process enables you to ensure the availability of materials. It is typically performed by the MRP controller who monitors the material shortage situation and solves any issues on time. Another main task is to ensure that sufficient supplies have been planned to cover requirements — whether from sales orders, stock transfer orders, or from production, for example. The goal is to ensure that both customer and production demand are available on time and to avoid any disruptions due to missing parts.

3.1.90. What is the purpose of "Production Control" in SAP S/4HANA Cloud 1902?

This process enables you to manage and regulate the manufacturing process. It is typically performed by the production supervisor who is responsible for dispatching production operations to individual machines if a work centre/resource has several alternative machines and for assigning shop floor specialists to operations or machines. The production supervisor also decides on measures to mitigate machine breakdowns or missing components, for example.

3.1.91. What is the purpose of "Production Execution" in SAP S/4HANA Cloud 1902?

This process enables you to make all the necessary preparations required for production and to document the production progress. It is typically performed by the shop floor specialist and includes the following tasks:

- Material staging before production starts.
- Reporting goods withdrawals.
- Processing time tickets for a production order or a process order.
- Entering the goods receipt information for the order on completion of the product.

3.1.92. What is the purpose of "Repetitive Manufacturing" in SAP S/4HANA Cloud 1902?

You can use Repetitive Manufacturing for planning and controlling your production in repetitive manufacturing and flow manufacturing environments. In repetitive manufacturing, you can plan and monitor the material flow in a much higher level of detail than that at which you collect and analyse costs. You use planned orders to model, plan, and trigger material flow and product cost collectors to collect the costs. Planned orders are simple and easy to manage with low overhead which you can use to model small increments of the production quantity. The product cost collectors collect the costs of the complete quantity produced during an accounting period. All deviations are aggregated. On the other hand, in discrete manufacturing, you plan and manage both the material flow and costs on the same level of detail in the production order, for example. Therefore, if you want to collect scrap and other deviations in detail, you are recommended to use discrete manufacturing.

3.1.93. What is the purpose of "Make-to-stock production" in SAP S/4HANA Cloud 1902?

Production is controlled without a direct reference to the sales order. Run schedule quantities determine the dates and quantities. Run schedule quantities are planned orders of the type PE that do not have to be released and that you do not have to convert into production or process orders to be able to carry out production. The requirements are generated by demand management, for example. Sales order quantities are delivered from stock and consume the planned independent requirement quantities in demand management, according to the planning strategy you select. A product cost collector is used to collect actual data and to settle costs.

3.1.94. What is the purpose of "Make-to-order production" in SAP S/4HANA Cloud 1902?

The system creates one or several planned orders which directly reference the sales order item. The material is then manufactured on the basis of these planned orders. That is, production is triggered by the receipt of the sales orders. For component materials that are relevant to repetitive manufacturing, you use the product cost collector of the component to collect costs. On finished item level, you either use valuated or non-valuated material: Costs are collected by the sales order if you use non-valuated material and by the product cost collector if the material is valuated.

3.1.95. What is the purpose of "Planning table" in SAP S/4HANA Cloud 1902?

Your main planning tool in repetitive manufacturing is the planning table. It is an operative planning tool that you can use to plan the production quantities. In the planning run, the system assigns the run schedule quantities to the correct line as defined in the production version. In the planning table, you can change the assignment of run schedule quantities to production lines/versions manually. In this type of manufacturing, you plan and control your production using the planning table based on periods and quantities. You can check production quantities, monitor the available capacity of the production lines and check up on the availability situation of the products produced on each line. In the planning table, you can enter and change production quantities and you can assign and reassign quantities to alternative production lines. The planning table allows you to schedule planned orders to the corresponding production lines.

3.1.96. What is the purpose of "Staging materials using the pull list" in SAP S/4HANA Cloud 1902?

You can use the pull list to control the in-house flow of material for supplying production with materials. A prerequisite for this is that the components required for production are already available (either produced in-house or procured externally) and must only be brought from their current storage location to the production storage location. The pull list checks the stock situation at the production storage location and calculates the quantities of missing parts. You can create replenishment elements for these missing parts. You can stage the components by direct stock transfer or stock transfer reservation. You can also trigger replenishment by setting a Kanban to empty or by creating transfer requirements in Warehouse Management.

3.1.97. What is the purpose of use of "Kanban" in SAP S/4HANA Cloud 1902?

Kanban is a procedure for controlling production and material flow based on physical material stock in production. Material that is required on a regular basis is kept available in small quantities in production. With Kanban, the replenishment or production of a material is only triggered when a certain quantity of the material has been consumed. This replenishment is triggered directly by production using previously maintained master data. Entries in the system are reduced to a minimum and all other actions are carried out automatically in the background. With Kanban, the production process is designed to control itself and the manual posting effort is kept to a minimum. Thus, you can achieve shorter lead times and reductions in stock levels. With Kanban, for example, the signal for material replenishment is triggered by the work centre that requires the material (the consumer or the demand source). This signal can simply be a card that the demand sources sends to the work centre that produces the material (producer or supply source). This card describes the required material, quantity, and information on where it is to be delivered. It is these cards, which are known as Kanban's in Japanese, that have given this type of production its name. Compared to the basic Kanban process that only uses boxes and cards to trigger material replenishment, this automated solution offers the following advantages:

- Goods movements are posted automatically meaning that inventory information is always up to date.
- Your supply sources are informed faster about the requirements situation at the demand source.
- The system collects data about the Kanban cycle times that you can use to improve the process.

3.1.98. What is the purpose of "Outsourced Manufacturing" in SAP S/4HANA Cloud 1902?

Basic subcontracting provides you with the means to instruct a supplier or subcontractor to process a material for which you provide the components. When procuring materials externally, you use subcontracting purchase orders or schedule lines to alleviate capacity bottlenecks. Subcontracting purchase orders/schedule lines instruct your subcontractor to make a certain finished material using the components that you provide and potentially using additional components provided by the subcontractor.

3.1.99. What is the purpose of "Basic External Processing" in SAP S/4HANA Cloud 1902?

Basic external processing provides you with the means to instruct a supplier or subcontractor to process individual production steps such as operations or sub-operations. The external processing of production order operations is frequently used for standardized process steps such as galvanizing which you cannot perform in your own factory. In the case of galvanizing, you may have environmental reasons for outsourcing this step to your subcontractor. In this case, it does not matter to the subcontractor which material IDs are produced. The subcontractor is only responsible for processing (galvanizing) a certain quantity of (metal) pieces.

3.1.100. What is the purpose of "Quality Planning" in SAP S/4HANA Cloud 1902?

Quality planning helps you to ensure the quality of your products, processes, and services right from the start. During the early stages of product design and development, it is important to have the correct quality tools and to implement appropriate quality-planning strategies in your processes.

3.1.101. What is the purpose of "Inspection planning" in SAP S/4HANA Cloud 1902?

You use the inspection planning functions to define inspection criteria (for example, material to be inspected, how the inspection is to take place, characteristics to be inspected).

3.1.102. What is the purpose of "Quality Inspection" in SAP S/4HANA Cloud 1902?

Quality management deals with quality inspection activities in procurement, in manufacturing, in stock handling processes, and in sales.

3.1.103. What is the purpose of "Quality Improvement" in SAP S/4HANA Cloud 1902?

Quality Improvement provides tools that form the basis for improving your processes and products. You can gain better insights into your inspection-related data, which helps you reach your quality goals.

3.1.104. What is the purpose of "Customer Project Management" in SAP S/4HANA Cloud 1902?

These features enable your project manager to create, manage, and monitor customer projects and internal projects. Project managers plan work packages and efforts, staff resources, and create billing plans for services. Subsequently, when efforts have been recorded, project managers can release billing proposals, which are later used in the creation of invoices. Project managers can also monitor projects for financial performance, using criteria such as cost, revenue, margin, and variance.

3.1.105. What is the purpose of "SAP Jam Collaboration" in SAP S/4HANA Cloud 1902?

For collaboration purposes, you can use the SAP Jam social software platform. You can achieve better team engagement where all project team members can drive and coordinate planning, implementation, and project execution.

3.1.106. What is the purpose of "Project Financial Control" in SAP S/4HANA Cloud 1902?

Managing projects, such as developing new products or running new investment projects, requires controlling related financial aspects. With Project Financial Control, you can define projects and its underlying elements to serve as accounting structures for subsequent project financial accounting tasks such as cost planning, actual cost and revenue collection or settlement.

3.1.107. What is the purpose of "Product Structure Management" in SAP S/4HANA Cloud 1902?

Product structure management can be used in early development phases. Product structures consist of a set of hierarchically ordered objects with the purpose of documenting one product or a set of similar products. They use abstract representations of products and components.

3.1.108. What is the purpose of "Sales Master Data Management" in SAP S/4HANA Cloud 1902?

You can use sales master data management to improve sales processes with accurate, structured, and accessible master data.

3.1.109. What is the purpose of "Price Management" in SAP S/4HANA Cloud 1902?

You can use price management to improve sales processes with accurate, structured, and accessible master data.

3.1.110. What is the purpose of "Sell from stock" in SAP S/4HANA Cloud 1902?

You use this feature to enable your internal sales representatives to enter a sales order based on customer requirements. When your internal sales representative creates or changes sales orders, the system confirms dates and quantities. Your internal sales representative can display and change the sales order to respond to customer questions. Your shipping specialist creates the delivery for the sales order and prints the picking list. Your internal sales representative can check the status of sales orders and resolve issues that stop sales orders from being fulfilled. The shipping specialist can view delivery details such as the picked delivery parts, the weight and volume of the delivery, the picking status, and so on. Your billing clerk creates an invoice for the delivery from the billing due list. The billing clerk displays the billing document in a list, checks the status of the billing document, posts the billing document, and sends output to the customer. The system transfers the billing document to the accounts receivable accountant. The accounts receivable accountant is then responsible for receiving payment for the billing document.

3.1.111. What is the purpose of "Credit management" in SAP S/4HANA Cloud 1902?

You use this feature to set credit limits for your customers. The system checks the credit limit when you create or change sales documents. If you change quantities or values in a document, the check is repeated. The system totals the receivables, the open items, and the credit value of the sales order for every item of a sales document. The system displays information about what caused blocks. When your credit department manually reviews the customer's current credit situation and when the sales order is approved, the system removes the block from the sales order.

3.1.112. What is the purpose of "Inquiry processing" in SAP S/4HANA Cloud 1902?

You can use this feature to enable your customer to request a quotation or sales information without obligation. An inquiry can relate to materials or services, conditions, and if necessary, delivery dates. The sales area that accepts the inquiry becomes responsible for providing a quote.

3.1.113. What is the purpose of "Contract processing" in SAP S/4HANA Cloud 1902?

You use this feature to create, change, display, and list contracts. You can list incomplete contracts, completed contracts, expiring contracts, and expired contracts.

3.1.114. What is the purpose of "Consignment processing" in SAP S/4HANA Cloud 1902?

You use this feature to enable a vendor (that is, an external supplier) to manage a stock of materials at the customer site (that is, the purchaser site). The vendor retains ownership of the materials until they are withdrawn from the consignment stores. Payment for consignment stock is required only when the material is withdrawn for use. For this reason, the vendor is informed of withdrawals of consignment stock on a regular basis.

3.1.115. What is the purpose of "Sales Billing" in SAP S/4HANA Cloud 1902?

You can create and manage billing documents, post them to financial accounting, and output them to a variety of channels. You can also create and manage billing-related documents such as invoice lists, preliminary billing documents, and billing document requests.

3.1.116. What is the purpose of "Omnichannel convergent billing" in SAP S/4HANA Cloud 1902?

You can use convergent billing to converge billing data from different categories of billing due list items (such as sales orders, outbound deliveries, and debit memo requests) to create combined, single invoices for customers. You can use omnichannel convergent billing to converge billing data from your SAP S/4HANA Cloud system with billing data from one or more external sources. The external billing data is persisted in your system in the form of external billing document requests (EBDRs). You can create EBDRs automatically by integrating external systems that send billing data, or you can create them manually by uploading billing data stored in spreadsheet files. EBDRs are added to the billing due list, from where they can be converged with your other billing due list items to create combined, single invoices for customers. Stand-alone billing of EBDRs is also possible.

3.1.117. What is the purpose of "Service Contract Management" in SAP S/4HANA Cloud 1902?

You can process external service contracts from a customer service manager's perspective. These service contracts are provided through the use of a corresponding API. Service contracts are outline agreements with business partners that define the services offered for a particular period. A service contract usually represents a long-term service agreement with customers. It defines the content and scope of services guaranteed within specific tolerance limits for certain parameters, for example, within predefined time frames.

3.1.118. What is the purpose of "Service Order Management" in SAP S/4HANA Cloud 1902?

You can process external service orders and service confirmations from a customer service manager's perspective. These service orders and confirmations are provided through the use of corresponding APIs.

A service order is a short-term agreement between a service provider and a service recipient, and it contains the relevant information for the specific service process. Service confirmations are used to confirm service orders.

3.1.119. What is the purpose of "Self-Service Requisitioning" in SAP S/4HANA Cloud 1902?

Self-service requisitioning allows you to create, manage, and track your orders efficiently. You can create items from external catalogues and free-text items. After ordering the products you require, an item or header-based approval process is triggered. Once your purchase requisition has been approved, a purchase order is created.

3.1.120. What is the purpose of "purchase requisition" in SAP S/4HANA Cloud 1902?

A purchase requisition is a request to procure a certain quantity of a material, or a service, so that it is available at a certain point in time. A purchase requisition is used as the starting point in purchasing and can trigger an approval process. A demand from an MRP run, for example, can result in a purchase requisition.

3.1.121. What is the purpose of "Purchase Order" in SAP S/4HANA Cloud 1902?

A purchase order is a request or instruction to an external supplier to deliver a specific quantity of materials at a certain point in time, or to perform services within a specific period.

3.1.122. What is the purpose of "Purchase Order Collaboration" in SAP S/4HANA Cloud 1902?

SAP S/4HANA Cloud supports the integration with business networks or external systems (currently the Ariba Network) to enable you to collaborate with your suppliers on purchase orders. You can do this by exchanging purchase-order-related messages between SAP S/4HANA Cloud and the business network or external system.

3.1.123. What is the purpose of "Supplier classification and segmentation" in SAP S/4HANA Cloud 1902?

Supplier classification and segmentation is an ongoing process in which you assess and classify your suppliers at regular intervals and allocate your suppliers to segments of different importance. You can then focus especially on those suppliers that are strategically important and critical to your business, thus enabling you to develop and manage your business relationships.

3.1.124. What is the purpose of "Inventory Management" in SAP S/4HANA Cloud 1902?

Inventory management covers the following tasks:

• Management and optimization (that is, the recording and tracking) of stocks of materials on a quantity and value basis
• Planning, entry, and documentation of stock movements such as goods receipts, goods issues, physical stock transfers, and transfer postings on daily basis
• Performance of physical inventory (stocktaking) and stock adjustments on periodical basis Inventory management is mainly performed by employees managing the company's stocks at plant and storage location level.

3.1.125. What is the purpose of "Delivery Management" in SAP S/4HANA Cloud 1902?

Delivery management is an important part of the logistics chain in which guaranteed customer service and distribution planning support play major roles. In delivery processing, all delivery procedure decisions can be made at the start of the process by doing the following:

• Taking into account general business agreements with your customer
• Recording special material requests
• Defining shipping conditions in the sales order. The result is an efficient and largely automatic shipping process in which manual changes are only necessary under certain circumstances.

3.1.126. What is the purpose of "Outbound Deliveries" in SAP S/4HANA Cloud 1902?

You can create outbound deliveries from a list of sales documents by manually starting a collective run or by scheduling a job to run in the background. You can also display logs with information related to your sales orders or deliveries. Additionally, a pick list can be automatically printed in the background and you can use this list to help you locate and pick goods for your delivery.

Depending on the current goods issue status, you can either post or reverse the goods issue. If the entries in the list have a different goods issue status, you can still select them for posting or for goods issue reversal. The system keeps track of which entries are candidates for which action and applies the respective actions only on the list entries with a status that matches the particular action.

You can analyse outbound delivery logs, that is, you can check the system messages that have been logged during the collective creation run of the outbound deliveries, either with or without success. In case of a failed delivery, it is up to you to correct the issues that are mentioned in the log and then create a new delivery for the respective sales order.

For each delivery log, you can look up the messages that the system has logged during the creation run. These messages can be related to a sales order, an individual delivery item, or to a delivery as a whole. You can also find out the numbers of the deliveries that the system has created.

3.1.127. What is the purpose of "Available to Promise" in SAP S/4HANA Cloud 1902?

Internal sales representatives and order fulfilment managers require mechanisms to configure, execute and monitor availability checks and optimize the distribution of supply. This is particularly important when the availability of materials needed to confirm requirements is limited.

You can use the available-to-promise (ATP) capabilities to confirm on which date and in which quantity a requirement can be fulfilled.

3.1.128. What is the purpose of "Warehouse Management" in SAP S/4HANA Cloud 1902?

Warehouse Management provides support with and real-time transparency into managing and processing material movements flexibly in a warehouse with its own stock.

3.1.129. What is the purpose of "Transportation Management" in SAP S/4HANA Cloud 1902?

Transportation Management (TM) supports transportation planning and execution in SAP S/4HANA Cloud in an order-based transportation consolidation scenario. Sales-order-based transportation demand (freight units) is built considering transportation constraints. Afterwards it is sent to a decentral transportation management system (TM system).

The planning result is received in SAP S/4HANA Cloud from the decentral TM system as freight orders. You can then trigger the creation of deliveries based on the consolidation information.

3.1.130. What is the purpose of "Freight agreement management" in SAP S/4HANA Cloud 1902?

You can use this feature to create and maintain freight agreements as the basis for calculating transportation charges billable to you by your carrier. You use freight agreements, along with calculation sheets, rate tables, and scales, to efficiently manage long-term contracts with your carriers.

3.1.131. What is the purpose of "Master Data Governance" in SAP S/4HANA Cloud 1902?

Master Data Governance enables you to adjust your master data quickly to reflect legal changes and respond flexibly to new requirements and to business transactions such as takeovers of other companies.

Master data consolidation provides an understanding of enterprise master data that is owned and maintained de-centrally. Master data consolidation delivers capabilities to load master data and to detect duplicates. For each of the resulting match groups, Master data consolidation calculates a best record out of the duplicates in that group, using survivorship rules on the master data attributes. The best records can be used in dedicated analytical or business scenarios.

Mass processing enables you to update multiple master data records at a time. To update records, you select the fields and records you want to change. Once you have made your changes, the system provides statistics on the changed fields and validates the data for use in business transactions before activating the changes.

3.1.132. What is the purpose of "Managing Contexts" in SAP S/4HANA Cloud 1902?

Contexts form the foundation of a legal transaction and can predefine settings for legal transactions that support a more standardized processing. You define a context that predefines how a legal transaction has to be processed; what information has to be provided; which parties are involved; which workflow steps are required; which documents are mandatory and so on.

3.1.133. What is the purpose of "Managing Legal Transactions" in SAP S/4HANA Cloud 1902?

Legal transactions are created based on a legal content request and is used to manage the legal content through its lifecycle. For this, the legal transaction collects all the information and material that is connected with the legal content: the parties involved in the creation of the legal content internally as well as externally, the deadlines that need to be observed, the tasks that need to be completed, and the documents that need to be generated in the process or are linked to the legal transaction.

3.1.134. What is the purpose of "Requesting Legal Content" in SAP S/4HANA Cloud 1902?

You can submit a request for legal content. You are guided through a process of providing required information for a specific business scenario. Based on this information, the system creates a legal transaction that is then used by the responsible teams, for example, Legal or Commercial, Compliance, Procurement to create the legal content and to manage the lifecycle of legal content as part of a business transaction or a business scenario.

3.1.135. What is the purpose of "Managing Categories" in SAP S/4HANA Cloud 1902?

Categories classify business objects such as contexts and legal transactions. You can use categories to classify legal content. Legal content is created by or exchanged between legal departments. Based on the categories that are assigned to the legal content business objects, the legal content can be classified.

3.1.136. What is the purpose of "Legal Content Overview" in SAP S/4HANA Cloud 1902?

Legal Content Overview analyses the most important legal transactions, contexts, and documents that you need to process. The graphical representation of the most critical tasks summarizes key information from the underlying apps that you are working on, so that you can analyse and identify upcoming important dates, reminders, and transactions and take quicker decisions. There are various actionable cards showing vital information ranked as per their expiration, risk or health.

3.1.137. What is the purpose of "Managing Legal Documents" in SAP S/4HANA Cloud 1902?

Documents are instances of legal content that are tailored to a specific transaction or activity in a certain business context. You can use legal documents that were uploaded as static files. You can download a document to edit, upload files, create versions of the documents, and manage the document attributes.

3.1.138. What is the purpose of "In-App User Assistance" in SAP S/4HANA Cloud 1902?

SAP S/4HANA Cloud supports the integration with an in-app user assistant (currently SAP Enable Now) to manage aspects of modern corporate learning.

When an in-app user assistant (for example, SAP Enable Now) is integrated, SAP S/4HANA Cloud supports you to connect content that is managed by the in-app user assistant.

3.1.139. What is the purpose of "Digital Assistance" in SAP S/4HANA Cloud 1902?

SAP S/4HANA Cloud supports the integration with a digital assistant (currently SAP CoPilot) to allow users to get their work done more efficiently.

3.1.140. What is the purpose of "Incident Management" in SAP S/4HANA Cloud 1902?

You can use the incident management solution for the recording of incidents, near misses, or safety observations available for all users. After the users make the recordings, the responsible manager can collect additional information from the people involved and report data internally or externally to fulfil legal, regulatory, and company reporting responsibilities, and define tasks for preventing further incidents.

3.1.141. What is the purpose of "Advanced Financial Closing (Entity Close)" in SAP S/4HANA Cloud 1902?

Entity Close allows you to define, automate, process, and monitor the entity close for your organization. It provides predefined task template sets covering financial closing activities for both month-end and year-end closing.

3.1.142. What is the purpose of "Corporate Close - Group Reporting" in SAP S/4HANA Cloud 1902?

Corporate Close allows you to prepare consolidated financial statements for group reporting, for both legal and management reporting purposes. This process offers a high degree of flexibility regarding the data collection process. You can highly integrate with the accounting features to automate the consolidation data collection process.

3.1.143. What is the purpose of "Advanced Compliance Reporting" in SAP S/4HANA Cloud 1902?

You use the advanced compliance reporting to get an optimized overview of your compliance reporting tasks, and to generate and send the compliance reports to the government on time. Advanced compliance reporting provides you with functional and configuration features. Users may use the features of advanced compliance reporting to process compliance reports in accordance with your compliance reporting requirements.

3.1.144. What is the purpose of "Advanced Credit Management" in SAP S/4HANA Cloud 1902?

The creditworthiness and payment behaviour of your "Business Partner(s)" can affect the business results of your company immediately.

3.1.145. What is the purpose of "Dispute Resolution" in SAP S/4HANA Cloud 1902?

Dispute resolution allows you to investigate and resolve dispute cases for open invoices.

3.1.146. What is the purpose of "Contract Accounting" in SAP S/4HANA Cloud 1902?

Contract Accounting provides the same functional scope as the Receivables Management and Payment Handling capability in LoB Sales.

3.1.147. What is the purpose of "Contract and Lease Management (CLM)" in SAP S/4HANA Cloud 1902?

Lease contracts describe contractual agreements between two partners: the lessor and the lessee. The lessor owns an asset, whereas the lessee has a right to use this asset during the period agreed in the lease contract. The lessee pays lease payments for the use of the asset, as agreed upon in the lease contract. SAP S/4HANA Cloud Contract and Lease Management provides a single point of entry for collection, validation of lease contract data, performs valuation calculations and generates the financial postings derived from these calculations. SAP S/4HANA Cloud Contract and Lease Management supports the requirements for the new IFRS 16 and US GAAP ASC 842 standard.

3.1.148. What is the purpose of "Cash Daily Operations" in SAP S/4HANA Cloud 1902?

Every day, cash managers need to perform tasks such as monitoring cash positions, making bank transfers, approving payments, pooling cash, and so on, to ensure the corporate functions and the business runs with sufficient fund.

3.1.149. What is the purpose of "Debt and Investment Management" in SAP S/4HANA Cloud 1902?

You can portray the process for managing your liabilities and capital investments. The following functional areas are covered: Front Office, Middle Office, Back Office, and Accounting. In addition, integrated posting and payment processes and integrated position reporting are available.

3.1.150. What is the purpose of "Manage Market Data" in SAP S/4HANA Cloud 1902?

You can use this feature to store the market data that you require for valuating and processing your financial transactions (such as FX rates, swap rates, reference interest rates, FX rate volatilities, credit spreads). For this, you can import market data.

3.1.151. What is the purpose of "Financial Risk Management" in SAP S/4HANA Cloud 1902?

You can deploy robust analytical functions that perform thorough checks for foreign exchange risks and counterparty risks. You can model a range of scenarios to gain insights into the extent of risks at the time of the analysis. The system provides support throughout the hedging process, from identifying risks and quantifying and analysing them through to hedging risks with hedging instruments. For financial transactions used as hedging instruments, the complete process is covered, from front office, middle office, and back office through to accounting.

3.1.152. What is the purpose of "Determine FX Risk Positions" in SAP S/4HANA Cloud 1902?

You can use this feature to collect future incoming and outgoing payments of your company that are associated with an FX risk. These payment flows are either actual payments that already have a fixed amount and time settings or they are only planned payments. This helps you to identify the risks in payment flows.

3.1.153. What is the purpose of "Hedge Management" in SAP S/4HANA Cloud 1902?

You can use this feature to gain an overview of the foreign exchange risk that your company is exposed to, as well as an overview of the financial instruments that you have used to mitigate that risk.

3.1.154. What is the purpose of "Determine Net Open Exposures" in SAP S/4HANA Cloud 1902?

You can use this feature to gain an overview of the FX risk that your company is exposed to as well as of the financial transactions that you used to mitigate that risk. It reports FX exposures and financial transactions (hedges) managed in Treasury and Risk Management. The net open exposures, that represent the unhedged portion of the FX exposures, and additional key figures are calculated, supporting you in making your hedging decisions.

3.1.155. What is the purpose of "Manage Correspondence for Financial Transactions" in SAP S/4HANA Cloud 1902?

You can create a correspondence document (confirmation/ deal slip) to be sent to your business partners/internal recipient via mail. Further, you can print the correspondence both automatically and manually.

3.1.156. What is the purpose of "Hedge Accounting" in SAP S/4HANA Cloud 1902?

It enables you to perform hedge accounting for cash flow hedges to support IFRS 9 requirements for the foreign exchange exposures that your company is exposed to including an automated designation process, which automatically designates hedging instruments into a hedging relationship when the financial transaction is saved, classification and reclassification process of designated hedging relationships as well as the de-designation process.

3.1.157. What is the purpose of "Manage Market Data" in SAP S/4HANA Cloud 1902?

You can use this feature to store the market data that you require for valuating and processing your financial transactions (such as FX rates, swap rates, reference interest rates, FX rate volatilities, or credit spreads). For this, you can import market data.

3.1.158. What is the purpose of "Integration with External Trading Platforms" in SAP S/4HANA Cloud 1902?

SAP S/4HANA Cloud supports the integration with external trading platforms (currently the treasury management integration for trading platforms application). SAP S/4HANA Cloud provides an interface that allows foreign exchange transactions traded on an external trading platform to be transferred to SAP S/4HANA Cloud. This enables seamless FX risk management processes as the key figures in SAP S/4HANA Cloud are automatically updated to reflect the traded amount.

3.1.159. What is the purpose of "Hybrid Treasury Deployment for Accounting" in SAP S/4HANA Cloud 1902?

SAP S/4HANA Cloud supports the transfer of accounting documents to an existing enterprise resource planning environment (currently SAP ERP Central Component). Treasury and Risk Management manages the financial transactions and generates the corresponding postings in SAP S/4HANA Cloud. These postings can be transferred to the financial accounting component in the enterprise resource planning system.

3.1.160. What is the purpose of "Treasury Payment Request Integration" in SAP S/4HANA Cloud 1902?

SAP S/4HANA Cloud supports you to generate and pay payment requests in central Financial Accounting component (currently either handled in an SAP S/4HANA system or an SAP ERP system). Treasury and Risk Management manages the financial transactions and triggers the payment request creation. The payment request is created in the central Financial Accounting component system either an SAP S/4HANA or SAP ERP system.

3.1.161. What is the purpose of "Treasury Workstation Cash Integration" in SAP S/4HANA Cloud 1902?

With the Treasury Workstation Cash Integration, you can deploy your SAP S/4HANA Cloud system as a Treasury Workstation and integrate with other business systems.

3.1.162. What is the purpose of "Demand-Driven Replenishment" in SAP S/4HANA Cloud 1902?

Demand-Driven Replenishment enables you to plan and manage supply chains based on customer demand, rather than through traditional MRP procedures. You can create the basis for a reliable material flow by defining buffers at strategically important points along a supply chain and by regularly adjusting the buffers' limits.

3.1.163. What is the purpose of "Resource Management" in SAP S/4HANA Cloud 1902?

SAP S/4HANA Cloud for resource management allows you, as a resource manager, to efficiently manage your resources while monitoring incoming resource requests at the same time. Resource management helps you to quickly find resources with free capacity and staff them for suitable projects. You can also find open resource requests and staff suitable resources for them.

3.1.164. What is the purpose of "Project Management" in SAP S/4HANA Cloud 1902?

Project Management enables you to monitor your internal projects, for example R&D projects, and to steer them through your company's organization. You are supported to keep all involved stakeholders in the loop about your ongoing projects, for example during the regular steering committee meetings.

3.1.165. What is the purpose of "Product Marketability and Chemical Compliance" in SAP S/4HANA Cloud 1902?

With the product marketability and chemical compliance solution you manage chemical compliance for your products across your organization. The features of this business solution support you to ensure product marketability and brand protection, and to reduce compliance costs. They enable you to manage regulatory requirements and compliance assessments of your product portfolio.

3.1.166. What is the purpose of "Dangerous Goods Management" in SAP S/4HANA Cloud 1902?

The dangerous goods management solution enables you to manage data that is needed to assess and classify products according to dangerous goods regulations. The solution also provides the classification information to the logistics chain, where the information can be used for transport checks.

3.1.167. What is the purpose of "Recipe and Formula Development" in SAP S/4HANA Cloud 1902?

You can use Recipe Development to maintain your ingredients, develop recipes and describe recipe processes. Recipes comprise information about the products and components of a process, the process steps to be executed, and the resources required for the production.

3.1.168. What is the purpose of "Handover to Manufacturing" in SAP S/4HANA Cloud 1902?

You can use this business process to create and update a manufacturing bill of material (BOM) using a recipe as data source. The creation or update of BOMs typically occurs when the development department has completed product and process definition, and this information has been finalized and approved for use in production. Guided Structure Synchronization automates this process, thereby enabling the user to keep development and manufacturing data aligned, reducing effort and improving data accuracy and consistency.

3.1.169. What is the purpose of "Classification" in SAP S/4HANA Cloud 1902?

The classification system allows you to use characteristics to describe various types of objects, and to group similar objects in classes – to classify objects, in other words, so that you can find them more easily later. You then use the classes to help you to find objects more easily, using the characteristics defined in them as search criteria.

This ensures that you can find objects with similar or identical characteristics as quickly as possible. Classes allow you to group objects together according to criteria that you define.
• You create classes for certain object types such as, for example, material.
• You use the class type to determine which object types can be classified in a class.
• You can assign characteristics to your class. These describe the objects that you classify in your class. When you assign a characteristic to a class, you can adapt (overwrite) the characteristic.

3.1.170. What is the purpose of "Document Management"?

Document Management (DMS) allows you to store, manage, and use documents during creating and maintaining digital product information company-wide and throughout the life cycle of a product. The following examples show some of the uses of document management in different areas of a company.

• In the design office, document management can be used to manage drawings. All design drawings can be linked to material masters.

• Companies that process complex documents can use document structures to organize these documents. All documents and texts that are logically connected can be grouped together in one document structure.

• A routing contains the sequence of operations for manufacturing a product. Documents can be allocated to the operations in a routing. These documents may be used, for example, to describe the specifications of a product, or to store inspection requirements.

• Documents can be linked to projects. You can use the document hierarchy to represent individual product folders that are given to the product administrators responsible.

3.1.171. What is the purpose of "Engineering Change Management" in SAP S/4HANA Cloud 1902?

Engineering change management is a central logistics function that can be used to change various aspects of production basic data (for example, bills of material, materials, and documents) with history (with date effectivity). All changes are made with reference to a change master record.

3.1.172. What is the purpose of "Embedded Systems Development" in SAP S/4HANA Cloud 1902?

Embedded systems development combines the development of embedded software and systems engineering. Embedded software is built-in computer software that runs on devices or machines. It provides functions along with various hardware and systems. You can define material types and document types for embedded software management. Embedded software requires a specific hardware and software environment to run accurately. You can manage and check compatibility information between embedded software and other parts of a product. As part of systems engineering, you can also link requirements to business objects involved in product lifecycle management.

3.1.173. What is the purpose of "Advanced Variant Configuration" in SAP S/4HANA Cloud 1902?

Variant configuration is for manufacturing complex products. Manufacturers often have to offer new variants of their products, and new variants can be created by modifying existing product designs as they process the order. The important thing is to react quickly to customers' requirements. The customer determines the features of the product. A customer buying a car, for example, can choose the features of the car and combine these features as required. The product configurator improves information exchange between sales, engineering, and production. Variant configuration helps the customer or salesperson to put together specifications for the product and ensure that the product can be produced from these specifications.

3.1.174. What is the purpose of "Product Structure Management" in SAP S/4HANA Cloud 1902?

Product structure management can be used in early development phases. Product structures consist of a set of hierarchically ordered objects with the purpose of documenting one product or a set of similar products. This is effective for high-volume, repetitive manufacturing, for example, in the automotive industry, as well as for complex machinery and equipment.

3.1.175. What is the purpose of "Convergent Invoicing" in SAP S/4HANA Cloud 1902?

Convergent Invoicing enables service providers to consolidate charges from one or more sources into a single invoice. The consolidated invoice may include charges from third parties. Providers thus have a complete view of the customer. They can see which party is responsible for any given charge. Convergent Invoicing enables providers to simplify and automate complex billing processes, making it easier to implement and monetize innovative services.

3.1.176. What is the purpose of "Receivables Management and Payment Handling" in SAP S/4HANA Cloud 1902?

Receivables Management and Payment Handling receives and manages large posting volumes, for example, created by billing processes, and uploads these postings to the general ledger. The software has been tailored towards the requirements of corporates across all industries and lines of business with high volumes of customers, subscriptions, and pay-per-use transactions. The processes provided with Receivables Management and Payment Handling are highly flexible to allow for a maximum of automation, as well as ensuring outstanding system performance and scalability. The collection process fully automates routine tasks such as the calculation of interest payments.

3.1.177. What is the purpose of "Integration with Machine Learning Intelligence" in SAP S/4HANA Cloud 1902?

SAP S/4HANA Cloud supports the integration with a machine learning system (currently SAP S/4HANA Cloud, intelligent insights for procurement) to allow users to optimize their procurement processes.

3.1.178. What is the purpose of "Central Procurement" in SAP S/4HANA Cloud 1902?

With Central Procurement, you can integrate your SAP S/4HANA Cloud system with some other enterprise resource planning systems in your system landscape (that is, SAP S/4HANA, SAP S/4HANA Cloud, or SAP ERP) to offer centralized procurement processes over your entire system landscape. SAP S/4HANA Cloud acts as a hub system and the enterprise resource planning systems act as connected systems in this integration scenario.

3.1.179. What is the purpose of "Central Requisitioning" in SAP S/4HANA Cloud 1902?

The Central Requisitioning scenario facilitates employees to have a unified shopping experience where they can create self-service requisitions in an SAP S/4HANA Cloud system (which acts as a hub system). They can, for example, select materials from the catalogues with desired sources of supply. This scenario also enables you to confirm the ordered goods in the hub system.

3.1.180. What is the purpose of "Central Purchase Contracts" in SAP S/4HANA Cloud 1902?

In an integrated procurement scenario, you can create central purchase contracts. These are global, long-term agreements between organizations and suppliers regarding the supply of materials or the performance of services within a certain period as per predefined terms and conditions. Central purchase contracts enable purchasers from various parts of a company in different locations to take advantage of the negotiated terms and conditions. Central purchase contracts are created in the SAP S/4HANA Cloud system (which acts as a hub system) and distributed to the connected systems, such as SAP ERP, SAP S/4HANA Cloud, or SAP S/4HANA.

3.1.181. What is the purpose of "Central Purchasing" in SAP S/4HANA Cloud 1902?

The Central Purchasing scenario provides a single point of access to display and manage purchasing documents centrally. The purchasing documents include purchase requisitions and purchase orders. These documents can be the ones that are created in the SAP S/4HANA Cloud system (which acts as a hub system) or the ones that have been extracted from the connected systems. SAP S/4HANA, SAP S/4HANA Cloud, or SAP ERP act as connected systems. Central Purchasing provides the flexibility of connecting multiple systems across an organization and carrying out procurement processes centrally.

3.1.182. What is the purpose of "Central Purchasing Analytics" in SAP S/4HANA Cloud 1902?

Central Purchasing Analytics provides users with centralized analyses and the necessary capabilities to better understand the procurement areas – both on a holistic level and on a more fine-granular level relating to connected systems. Strategic buyers can analyse the consumption of central contracts across entire organizations, as well as identify where global contracts are not being properly utilized. Additionally, monitoring the global purchasing spend using drill-down capabilities pinpoints the spend volume across the entire organization.

3.1.183. What is the purpose of "Integration with External Procurement Systems" in SAP S/4HANA Cloud 1902?

SAP S/4HANA Cloud supports the integration with external procurement systems (currently SAP Ariba and SAP Fieldglass) to combine the advantages of the integrated product with the integrated business processes and data transparency provided by SAP S/4HANA Cloud.

3.1.184. What is the purpose of "Integration of Central Procurement with External Procurement System " in SAP S/4HANA Cloud 1902?

SAP S/4HANA Cloud supports the integration of Central Procurement with an external procurement system (currently SAP Ariba) to combine the advantages of the integrated product with the advantages of a scenario where your professional purchasers can either operate centrally in SAP S/4HANA Cloud (acting as a hub system) or de-centrally in the connected systems.

3.1.185. What is the purpose of "Integration of Invoice Processing with Optical Character Recognition (OCR) Programs " in SAP S/4HANA Cloud 1902?

SAP S/4HANA Cloud supports the integration with OCR programs (currently OpenText) to enable processing of invoices that were converted from picture files into a structured format.

3.1.186. What is the purpose of "Advanced Available to Promise" in SAP S/4HANA Cloud 1902?

Internal sales representatives, order fulfilment managers and order fulfilment specialists require mechanisms to configure, execute and monitor availability checks and optimize the distribution of supply. This is particularly important when the availability of materials needed to confirm requirements is limited.

You can use the advanced available-to-promise (aATP) capabilities to confirm on which date and in which quantity a requirement can be fulfilled.

3.1.187. What is the purpose of SAP BW/4HANA?

SAP BW/4HANA has simplicity, openness, high performance and modern interface. It

- is a new data warehouse solution
- is highly optimized for HANA
- accelerates solution development
- means you have one single version of truth
- solves analytics problems in seconds that take other systems days
- is ready for the internet of things (IoT) at petabyte scale.

3.1.188. What is the version for SAP BW/4 HANA?

SAP BPC 11.0 version in S/4HANA 1902.

3.1.189. What is the purpose of "SAP S/4HANA Migration Cockpit" in SAP S/4HANA Cloud 1902?

The SAP S/4HANA migration cockpit facilitates the transfer of business data from a source system to an SAP S/4 HANA system. Source systems can be SAP systems and non-SAP systems. The SAP S/4HANA migration cockpit uses predefined migration objects to identify and transfer the relevant data.

To start the SAP S/4HANA migration cockpit logon to your SAP S/4HANA backend system with SAP GUI Logon.

To start the SAP S/4HANA Migration Cockpit you use transaction LTMC.
Note: For this transaction, your user needs role SAP_CA_DMC_MC_USER.

3.1.190. What is the SAP S/4HANA System Conversion tools?

a. ABAP test cockpit
b. SPAU
c. SPDD
d. SQL Monitor
e. Readiness check
f. SCMON
g. CCLM.

3.1.191. What is the purpose of "SAP Readiness Check and Simplification Item-Check (SI-Check)" tool?

The tools SAP Readiness Check and Simplification Item-Check (SI-Check) are used to support the conversion process.

Reference - SAP Note 2290622 (about the SAP Readiness Check).

3.1.192. What is the purpose of "Maintenance Planner" tool?

You have to use the Maintenance Planner to do the conversion to SAP S/4HANA. The Maintenance Planner generates the download files (add-ons, packages, DBDs, and the stack configuration file) that the Software Update Manager (SUM) uses to do the conversion. In particular, the Maintenance Planner checks if the following items are supported for the conversion:

● Add-ons to your system
● Active business functions in your system
● Industry solutions.

If there is no valid conversion path for any of the items listed above (for example, an add-on is not released for the conversion yet), the Maintenance Planner prevents the conversion. After the check, the Maintenance Planner creates the stack configuration file (stack.xml).

3.1.193. What is the purpose of "Software Update Manager (SUM)" tool?

Software Update Manager (SUM) is the technical tool used for the system conversion to SAP S/4HANA.

3.1.194. What is ABAP Unit?

ABAP unit is the official xUNIT testing framework for ABAP.

3.1.195. What are the features of ABAP Unit?

ABAP unit:

- Provides an environment for execution of unit tests in isolation
- Provides assertion-methods for testing expected results
- Tightly integrated into the programming language ABAP
- Production code and unit test code are bundled and transported together
- Now enhanced to support testing of other development objects like ABAP Core Data Services.

3.1.196. What is Blockchain?

Bitcoin
For verifying the transfer of funds, operating independently of a (central) bank cryptocurrency encryption techniques are used.

Blockchain
Architectural concept that enables the decentralized, secure, direct, digital transfer of values and assets.

Distributed Ledger Technology
Distributed ledger consensus of replicated, shared digital data across various countries, sites or institutions. No central administrator or centralized data storage.

Blockchain is a new protocol for distributed ledgers in multi-party business processes. Blockchain can transform transactional networks.

3.1.197. What are the goals of HANA?

HANA Goals
- Enables New Application and Optimize Existing Application
- High Performance and Scalability
- Hybrid Data Management System
- Compatible with Standard DBMS feature
- Support for Text analysis, indexing and search
- Cloud support and application isolation
- Executing application logic inside the data layer.

3.1.198. What are the different building blocks of SAP Model Company services?

The following are the step-by-step building blocks of SAP Model Company services:

a. Foundation (industry reference architecture and digital business framework)
b. Accelerators (configuration and how-to guides, test demo scripts, and implementation tools)
c. Business content (business process hierarchy, end-to-end scenarios and process diagrams by roles)
d. Engineered services (hand-over and enablement workshops to jumpstart discovery, exploration or fit-gap analysis, and realization)
e. Preconfigured solutions (available as a ready-to-run appliance, including all applications, configuration, and sample data)

SAP Model Company offers end-to-end processes ranging from detailed business process master lists down to test scripts, along with industry and LoB best practices. In addition, all content is documented in SAP Solution Manager, and the services are covered by SAP Value Assurance service packages for SAP S/4HANA.

The services also include an embedded transformation road map, which supports clients in reducing cost, decreasing risk, and accelerating adoption during exploration (such as through proven fit-gap analysis), and realization activities.

3.1.199. For whom is SAP Model Company most suited?

SAP Model Company services are suited for companies that are looking at implementing a standardized SAP system in a short time frame. This approach fits customers new to SAP as well as long-term SAP customers looking at transforming their system landscape.

3.1.200. What are the main benefits observed among clients that are already utilizing the SAP Model Company Service offering?

The main benefits observed among clients that are already utilizing the SAP Model Company Service offering include:

o Speed of deployment (for example, reducing total discovery time from 65 to 15 days and delivery time from 24 down to 12 months)1
o Higher "fit to standard" (for example, reducing custom development efforts by >30%)2
o Ease and speed of decision making (demonstrated by a significantly decreased the number of meetings)3
o Future-proof foundation (for example, having the agility and flexibility to react to future changes and unlock innovation potential)
o Significantly improved project scoping (for example, enabling confident estimates on the amount of licenses needed).

NOTES

NOTES

Chapter 4 - GIT – Tips & Tricks

What is GIT?
- Distributed Version Control System (DVCS)
- Created by Linus Torvalds.

GIT Client & Server Tools

Git Client Tools: CLI, SourceTree, GITHUB desktop, GITGUI, Eclipse, Microsoft Visual Studio

GIT Server Tools: GITHUB, Bitbucket, GITLAB

Setting Up GIT

Download - https://git-scm.com/downloads
Setting Up GIT
git config —global user.name 'sudipta'
git config —global user.email 'sudipta@booleanminds.com' git config -l

GIT Config

-   Global Level

-   System Level

-   Repository Level.

GIT – Sample pseudo commands

• git cat-file -t <hash>

• git cat-file -p <hash>

• git cat-file -p <treehash>

• git cat-file -p <blobhash>

- **Config**
  - git config -l
  - git config --global --replace-all user.email 'parvezmisarwala@gmail.com'
  - git config - -global core.autocrlf true (in case of windows)
  - git config - -global core.autocrlf input (in case of mac and linux)
  - git config - -global core.autocrlf false (if only windows)
  - git config --global core.editor vim
  - git config core-sparsecheckout true (to checkout selected directory). Details below
  - git config - -global merge.tool kdiff3 (brew install kdiff3)
  - git mergetool -t kdiff3
  - git config - -global diff.tool kdiff3
  - git config --global core.whitespace -trailing-space,-space-before-tab - This will disable whitespace warnings
  - git config - -global clean.requireForce false

- **add, commit, amend**
  - git add .
  - git add -u - Stages only modified files and ignores untracked files
  - git add -i (for interactive staging)
  - git add file1.txt file2.txt file3.txt
  - git add *.txt
  - git add p
  - git rm —cached - To unstage
  - git reset HEAD <filename> - remove from staging
  - git commit
  - git commit -m <commit message>
  - git commit -am <commit message>
  - git commit - -amend
  - Exercise
    - 1. Create 4 files and commit these files in all separate commits
- Status
  - git status -u - Shows untracked files
  - git status -sb - Gives output in short format of your branch

- **.gitignore**
  - .gitignore - to share the ignore files
  - exclude - for local ignore
  - git check-ignore -v * - To list ignored files

- **status**
  - git status
  - git status -u : shows untracked files
  - git status -sb : gives output in short format of your branch

- **log**
  - git shortlog -s -n : To get the number of commits
  - git log -p
  - git log - -oneline
  - git log - -graph
  - git log --oneline --abbrev-commit --all --graph
  - git log - -stat: In each commit shows statistics for files modified
  - git log - -shortstat: From the --stat command.git displays only the changed/ insertions/deletions line
  - git log - -name-only: After the commit information shows the list of files modified.
  - git log - -name-status: Display the list of files affected with added/modified/deleted information as well.
  - git log --pretty=oneline
    - %H-Commit hash, %h-Abbreviated Commit hash
    - %T- Tree hash, %t-Abbreviated tree hash
    - %P-Parent hashes, %p-Abb.. parent hashes
    - %an-Author name, %ae-Author email, %ad-Author date, %ar-Author date relative
    - %cn-committer name, %ce-Committer email, %cd-Committer date, %cr-Relatives
    - %s: Subject (commit message)

- **Alias**
  - git config —global alias.co commit

- git config —globbal alias.last 'log -1 HEAD'
- git config --global alias.unstage 'reset HEAD —'

- **rm**
  - git rm - Remove files from the working tree and from the index
  - -q, --quiet   do not list removed files
  - --cached   only remove from the index (to untrack)
  - -n, --dry-run   dry run
  - -f, --force   override the up-to-date check
  - -r   allow recursive removal
  - --ignore-unmatch   exit with a zero status even if nothing matched

- **mv**
- manually renaming a file
- **clean** - Remove untracked file from working directory
  - git clean -f -n - Show what will be deleted with the -n option:
  - git clean -f -d - Also removes directories
  - git clean -f -X - Also removes ignored files
  - git clean -f -x - Removes both ignored and non-ignored files
  - git clean -i

- Revert - To undo a committed snap shop
- Reset - Reset Current head to specified state
  - Git reset --hard
    - Clean directory, no modified files
    - Modified files, not staged yet
    - Staged file, not committed yet
  - Git Reset --soft - Does not touch the index file or the working tree at all
    - Clean directory, no modified files
    - Modified files, not staged yet
    - Staged file, not committed yet
  - Git Reset - -mixed -Resets the index but not the working tree

- Clean directory, no modified files
- Modified files, not staged yet
- Staged file, not committed yet
- branch, merge, rebase, rebase -i, conflict, mergetool
  - View conflicted files
    - git diff --name-only —diff-filter=U
    - git ls-files -u | awk '{print $4}' | sort | uniq
    - git ls-files -u | cut -f 2 | sort -u
  - View if branch is merged or unmarked
    - git branch --merged master
    - git branch --no-merged master
  - Rebase
    - git rebase master
    - git rebase —onto
      - git rebase --onto master next topic
      - git rebase --onto topicA~5 topicA~3 topicA
    - git rebase -i
- **Patch**
  - git format-patch master --stdout > fix_empty_poster.patch : This will create a new file fix_empty_poster.patch with all changes from the current (fix_empty_poster) against master.
  - git apply --stat fix_empty_poster.patch: This will show commits which is present in path file
  - git am --signoff < fix_empty_poster.patch - This will apply the patch
  - git format-patch -10 HEAD --stdout > 0001-last-10-commits.patch: The last 10 patches from head in a single patch file:
  - git format-patch -1 <sha> --stdout > specific_commit.patch: To generate patch from a specific commit (not the last commit):
  - Apply Patch
    - Checkout to a new branch: $ git checkout review-new-feature
    - # If you received the patch in a single patch file: $ cat new-feature.patch | git am
    - # If you received multiple patch files: $ cat *.patch | git am

- cherrypick
  - To pick up a particular commit

- Stash
- remote
  - git remote
  - git remote -v
  - git remote show origin
  - git remote rename pb paul
  - git remote rm paul
  - git branch --set-upstream-to=upstream/foo foo
- Clone
- Sync Repository with Pull Push fetch merge and rebase
  - Pull - Updates the working directory

- Fetch and Merge
- tag
  - git tag v1.0 -m 'tag message'
  - git tag -l
  - git checkout v1.0 -b NewBranch

- submodules
  - A submodule allows you to keep another Git repository in a subdirectory of your repository.
  - Submodule does not automatically upgrade
  - The other repository has its own history, which does not interfere with the history of the current repository. This can be used to have external dependencies such as third party libraries for example.
    - git submodule add https://github.com/pmisarwala/myrepo1.git
    - cat .gitmodules
    - Clone a repo with submodule
      - git submodule update - -init
- **subtree**
  - Add a subtree: git subtree add --prefix .vim/bundle/fireplace https://github.com/tpope/vim-fireplace.git master —squash

- To update: git subtree pull --prefix .vim/bundle/fireplace https://github.com/tpope/vim-fireplace.git master --squash
- **Split** repository
    - git subtree split --prefix=lib -b split
- **symlinks**
    - ln -s originalfile linkedfile
    - git ls-files -s
    - git config - -system core.symlinks true

- **show**
    - git show <commit ID>: filename - This will show content of file for a particular commit
- help -a
- annotate, blame, br, ci
- citool, describe difftool
- Hooks

To Amend Last commit
- One method
    - git rebase —interactive '31f73c0^'
    - choose edit instead of default pick
    - make changes and do git add .
    - git rebase —continue
    - (This will update the current commit, but commit ID will be new)
- Second method (
    - make changes and do git add .
    - git commit —all —amend
- Third method
    - git rebase -i <commit ID> (edit)
    - update the contents..
    - git add .
    - git commit —amend
    - git rebase —continue

- Fourth Option
    - git reset HEAD~
    - git add …
    - git commit -c ORIG_HEAD

Visual Studio

- Git cherry-pick is supported in MS Visual Studio 2015 Update-2
- Submodules are supported in MS VS 2015 Update-2

Bitbucket Plugin Development

- Install Atlassian Plugin SDK
- Run command atlas-create-stash-plugin
    - com.atlassian.stash.plugin.demoplugin
    - demo-plugin
- Run command atlas-create-stash-plugin-module
    - 8
    - Democlass

NOTES

NOTES

NOTES

Chapter 5 - Test your knowledge

1. Mention most common challenges faced by your Agile teams.

2. In Agile, is it fair for a customer to ask for expected completion date for a new work item (user story)?

3. Do we accept changes within a sprint, or not? If we do, won't it disrupt our sprint plan that is in progress? And, if we don't, would we be less of an 'agile' team?

4. Mention Kanban myths and misconceptions.

5. Mention Agile myths and misconceptions.

6. What are the common Agile mistakes?

7. What are the common KANBAN mistakes?

8. How do you decide the sprint length for a team?

9. In Agile what are the common estimation techniques?

10. How many planning you are doing in SCRUM?
11. How to reduce technical debt (improving depth of testing, test driven development)?

12. Explain DoR (definition of Ready) and implementation thereof in each sprint?

13. Explain DoD (definition of Done) and implementation thereof in each sprint?

14. Explain UAT before delivery of each sprint in a production environment for integration/testing?

15. Explain "Definition of Ready" (DoR) vs. "Definition of Done" (DoD)?

16. Explain "Agile Estimation and Planning"?

17. Explain critical success factors on PULL mechanism adoption on Agile team rather then PUSH?

18. How team will calculate and optimize Sprint length where 190 team members are working from different geographies' using SCRUM OF SCRUMS?

19. Explain some case studies on successful E2E transformation of Waterfall teams to Agile Teams?

20. Explain some business cases of increasing ROI from business front?

21. Explain common Agile product development Myths?

22. Explain different techniques on backlog prioritization?

23. Explain "Agile Manifesto Myths"?

24. Explain "Turnaround time for a Story"? In Agile, is it fair for a customer to ask for expected completion date for a new work item (user story)?

25. Should we allow Changes within Sprint?
Do we accept changes within a sprint, or not? If we do, won't it disrupt our sprint plan that is in progress? And, if we don't, would we be less of an 'agile' team?

26. Explain "SAP Activate Methodology" - "Agile way to deliver Cloud based
SAP S/4 HANA Greenfield and Brownfield projects -Creating disruption in 21st Century's Worldwide business Model"?

27. Explain common challenges facing by 1000 members SCRUM of SCRUM teams working in 5 different Countries?

28. How we can introduce Machine learning and Artificial intelligence in Agile approach of delivering Projects?

29. How we can introduce blockchain in Agile approach of delivering Projects?

30. Is PMO role required in Agile Projects?

31. Explain "Less vs. Scrum @Scale vs. Nexus vs. SAFe vs. DAD in scaling Agile"?

32. Explain RPA (Robotic process automation) in Agile?

33. Explain common Agile mistakes?

34. Explain Yogi requirements from Atlassian?

35. Explain Reiki Practices for Agile Teams?

36. Explain Agile DNA?

37. Explain SPRINT Retrospectives Myths?

38. Explain SPRINT Planning Myths?

39. Explain SPRINT Review Myths?

40. Explain Daily stand-up meeting Myths?

41. Explain different ways to increase SCRUM Teams velocity?

42. Explain challenges in Application platform upgrade in Agile way?

43. Can we measure Productivity of each team member working in SCRUM Project, how? If not, why?

44. How to engage business in Agile transformation?

45. How to improve team engagement and motivation of the team members?

46. How to coach tough, high attitude and high ego team members?

NOTES

NOTES

NOTES

NOTES